The Answer To All You Desire Is Within You... You Are Worthy

Shona Ann Hill

Always follow Your Inner Guidance and fully Discover You and Your Magnificence through it.

S. A. Hill

BALBOA.
PRESS

A DIVISION OF HAY HOUSE

"Photography by: Nik Pickard of Nik Pickard Photography,
also within Dannie Lea. Micklegate, York, UK."

Balboa Press books may be ordered through booksellers or by contacting:

Balboa Press
A Division of Hay House
1663 Liberty Drive
Bloomington, IN 47403
www.balboapress.com
1 (877) 407-4847

Print information available on the last page.

ISBN: 978-1-5043-5252-9 (sc)
ISBN: 978-1-5043-5254-3 (hc)
ISBN: 978-1-5043-5253-6 (e)

Library of Congress Control Number: 2016904203

Balboa Press rev. date: 5/18/2016

I dedicate this book to my dear friend and mentor Lorraine Turner. Thank you for always seeing me and believing in me. Your encouragement has driven me to truly shine my truth and fly. Thank you for being you.

Chapter One

I am going to start this book with an honest heartfelt truth for everyone who reads it. That is … You are so worthy and deserving of everything you have ever seen and envisioned for yourself. Even more importantly, ALL… YES every single person on this beautiful earth is capable of achieving it, regardless of background, colour, creed or any other obstacle that we wonderful humans choose to put in our way.

One of the golden secrets of achieving your dreams is following your intuitive feelings from the heart, your gut instincts. For example, I am writing this book for you, and it is a heartfelt desire to do so, and intuitively guided. However, I did have all that "mind talk" come in saying, "you aren't good enough", "you won't finish it", "someone else will do it before you, so you may as well not bother"… You know the thoughts I am talking about, those wonderful human hindrances that we choose to give ourselves… aren't we wonderfully delightful?

Believe it or not, all those emotions that do not stem from "LOVE", like fear, anger; those "I can do that better than them" thoughts… they all stem from the ego… otherwise known as Kali.

Many humans make the mistake of thinking that the ego is all about being pompous, and thinking you are better than everybody else. In its fullness it is so much more. Kali/ego is all those emotions that can hinder us on our progress forward. Anger, fear, jealousy, procrastination; they all come from Kali. They can rise up from nowhere like an ugly monster, to hinder our progress towards our dreams. Kali rises when we do not have trust and belief in who we are. It also shows us all our old patterns of behaviour, and things we have picked up from others along our journey. We find all our faults through Kali rising, and sometimes then can project them out onto other people. Kali is powerful, but never more powerful than the pure honest real truth that is found in your heart. Kali is all about human emotion, whereas the heart is about feelings, and is your soul's guidance towards your dreams in life.

When we come from the heart, the emotions associated with Kali do not exist; they simply aren't there, and everything flows to and from us in divine ease and grace. So why are they there? The truth is to push us to go for our goals and desires, to overcome all obstacles, and achieve all that we are given in divine intuitive guidance from source.

Many of us make the mistake of believing that we are humans with a soul. This is where we can make the mistake of letting the "mind talk" override the "heart talk", and get stuck in the humdrum of physical life as a consequence. The divine truth of the situation is that we are souls experiencing human existence. In that realisation everything is immediately turned on its head and a wonderful divine shift of consciousness takes place.

You are in fact an infinite and an unlimited being of unconditional love; here to spread your own personal message. Acknowledge and take a deep breath into the abdomen, breathe in the wisdom of source that you are, and know that you are simply housed in a wonderful casing of your souls devising. There is no one else in this world like you, and there never will be again. What you contain within you is unique to you. ALL those childhood dreams that you had, and often openly shared in play with all, are in fact what you are meant to be doing. All those times you have said "Oh I would really love to do...".... well DO IT, simply because you can. As a soul having human experience, there are no boxes. You can do anything that your heart feels is right, and puts forward to you. Even more importantly, if you follow through the intuitive guidance of the heart, you will be abundant in all areas of your life, and experience unabashed joy and playful happiness always.

Chapter Two

∽

We all go through "tough times" as humans. In truth though, they never happen to drag us down, and make us feel that we aren't meant to achieve our dreams. They actually happen to take us closer to them. They simply exist to teach us all that we need to fulfil our dreams on all levels. This is how we need to start looking at our so called "challenges".

This I am sure has brought up the thought pattern of "How do I do that?"…

The word "How" creates such blocks to our progress as humans. This is because we are trying to take control of the situation. Where Source is in the equation, otherwise known as God, there is only flow. There is a divine plan, and it isn't our place to decide the "how" of how things take place, as quite frankly, they are already taken care of by God.

It isn't our place to take control; it is our place to follow our hearts intuitive guidance. If your heart leaps in joy, the answer is yes, if it feels nothing that excites it, then the answer is no. Both responses are extremely powerful, with extremely powerful effects. The feelings in the heart make dreams come true, if you choose to listen and follow them. This is where the answers to ALL you desire, and every single question that you have lies; in the heart. It is about having a loving perspective on everything that happens to you. Yes, you will get "brain talk" coming into the equation, we are having a human experience after all, and that is what humans do. The trick is to go within and listen to your intuitive feelings of heart, your gut instincts. As humans that have got used to experiencing, the "humdrum" of human life, this may initially not be as easy as it appears on the pages of this book.

If you are one of those that experiences "mind talk", one of the many ways to combat it, is through the breath. Our souls have been so wise in their creating of us, that they have given us everything that we require to heal as a natural thing we experience. The truth is the breath is tremendously healing. Every time an intuitive creation comes to you, as soon as the mind starts popping up blocks for you, take a deep breath into the abdomen, breathing in the love of the heart, and breathe out the thoughts of hindrance. This is all that is required. However, as humans we can be impatient with such activities, and this is why people, such as myself, are here to help you achieve your hearts desires, and the life you have always envisioned for yourself. Those connected to the fact that we are souls having human experience, see solutions where others may only be seeing the problem, and finding it difficult to get beyond that space. When you are in this space of finding it difficult to move forward, I am here along with many others to assist you, and always will be no matter what the problem. A solution will always be seen, as the spiritual leaders of the world are all already seeing. Here lies something that you are required to learn. What I am you are too, as we are all energetically connected in the consciousness of all that is.

Every single human being is so precious and uniquely gifted, and you are here to simply shine your gifts out to the rest of us. This is so all of humanity can have the possibility to learn and grow from what you know, and achieve everything that we have always wanted for ourselves. We are all equal, and no one is more important than another. We each have our place to fill in the divine picture, and we are all here to simply BE in peace and harmony, and work together as a collective, to repair and heal the world. All we need to do to achieve this is "shine" all that we are in love from the heart. In that space there is no wrong, and simply compassionate understanding of all people, situations and circumstances. This is what we are working towards… that perfect world which we are always talking about. The wonderful thing about it too, is that the answers to it aren't found in relying on those outside ourselves, which appear to be in places of influence, the answers are within us. Each and every one of us can create our own perfect world by simply going to our heart and listening to its guidance. The souls that we are, are extremely wise and all knowing, and in full connection with them, we simply cannot in any way go wrong.

In the knowledge that everything that we require to achieve the perfect envisioned life for us is within, then we must stop being influenced by outside things. Stop watching and reading the news. It has got into a space of spreading fear, and all those emotions that hinder our progress in truth and heart. If you are reading this and create the news or a newspaper, look for POSITIVE things to report… The way to change what is happening in the world is to focus on positive things, the things that we want and are intuitively guided to us, rather than to report that which does not serve and spreads fear… Share positive tidings only, and follow positive feelings and messages from within. This is the way forward.

When people come to see me, they tend to focus on things that are happening outside of them, the created "mind talk" illusion, rather than what they really want for them. They talk about all that is going on outside of them, some are even stressed and disorientated with it all, even said to be "depressed".

What actually does "depressed" mean?

Well, it is the pushing down of all that is your truth and who you are, and trying to be or become everyone else's picture of you... If this is you then please stop and recognise, you are beautiful exactly the way that you are, and there is no need whatsoever, to be anyone else's picture of you. You know what your unique qualities are. You know the voice within, and what it says about you and your truth and who you truly are. Listen and act upon that. You are not here to be someone you are not, to please other people. You are here purely and simply to be yourself and who you are. If someone is trying to make you something that you are not, or is trying to make you do something that, at that time doesn't feel right to you, move away from them, no matter who it is. It is perfectly ok to stand in your power and say no, if something doesn't feel right to you.

Actually, in all honesty, when people come to see me, and have finished talking about all the outside influences that are distressing them, when asked to focus just on themselves... guess what... all is well... There is absolutely nothing wrong with them at all in their own space. All their so called "issues", have come from other people, interfering in their space, or outside events that they have allowed themselves to get completely absorbed into. There is an important lesson here. Please stop allowing yourself to become other people's views of you. Please stop allowing situations nowhere near you to dictate your responses. These reactions are not you, never have been and never will be. Every single person that you meet, will see you differently. No one will see you the same way as anyone else. Pleasing one person will always disappoint someone else. What conclusion can be drawn from this? You are not anyone else's business, and they are none of yours. You will have friends that just see your love and strength of heart that will always be there for you to offer a listening ear, offer solutions to problems you relay, and spend fun times with you. But they do not need to take you or your life on board. Everyone exists to be in their own space and "shine" out their uniqueness to the rest of the world. Each person can find and own their own space for themselves, without any influence from another over it. To simply be in one's own space is an incredibly powerful and wise position.

Chapter Three

∾

When we purely and simply just focus on the self, nothing is wrong or out of place, and we nearly always are moving towards our hearts desires, or at the very least see the way to get there simply and easily with no issues. Of course "challenges", so to speak, may come up for us along the way, as not everyone has discovered this simple way of self-focus to ease stress levels. As long as we keep focused on our personal outcome, the challenges can be worked through and the solutions easily provide. Where one direction hasn't worked out, go within and listen to the heart, the voice of the soul, and find another route until that one comes back into play, if indeed that is meant to happen.

When I say "go within and listen to the heart", this can actually be summed up by one word... Meditation. By "meditation", I do not mean the stereotype of sitting still with your legs crossed and saying "Om". Although this can work, there are many ways that take you within to your heartfelt intuitive space. Yoga and Tai Chi for example, are forms of meditation. Anything that brings you to a balanced state of peace within is a form of meditation. Being in nature, by the sea, with animals, listening and creating music, are all examples of what can be classed as "meditation". Some even get their pearls of wisdom and inspiration in the shower, or through some form of exercise. So do what works for you to connect with yourself, and do it often.

The important thing to remember is that where one route doesn't provide fruit, another one will. This new route that provides, purely and simply will bring about better results, than what you ever envisioned from the route that stopped for whatever reason.

Hold true to yourself and your truth, and let all things come in and out around you, without any form of attachment. Do not hold on to anything that happens on the outside of you. If it hasn't worked it simply isn't meant to be. There is no point in trying to control and force the issue, as it simply will not work out for you. All it will do is keep you stuck and stagnant in a place that doesn't serve you.

What doesn't serve you, ultimately, will not serve anyone else either, so simply allow the person and/or the situation to leave you, and move on to the next intuitive message that comes. If something doesn't work out, it tends to show that agenda has come into the equation somewhere, and it has caused a block in proceedings, as it is disserving to all. Where there is heart, there is never any form of agenda, only playful pure innocent joy to help ourselves to grow, and ultimately aid all of humanity to grow in the process. Heartfelt genuineness is the way forward.

Chapter Four

~

We are moving into a "New Age" of being, where all old patterns of greed, agenda and self-serving ego no longer will bring any form of positive result. We are moving into a space where play that serves all is the way forward. This is a space where positivity is the result and love and compassionate unconditional beingness is what takes us forward. Karma no longer exists, as this loving self-caring intuitive state comes in for us.

How do we achieve this?

It is through being detached from situations. By that I do not mean being cold and unloving, on the contrary in fact. Detachment is all about honouring the self, and self-care. We can be LOVE through and through for all that come to us for assistance, but we do not need to become involved in it. What we can do is be there for the person, see the solution that will take them forward, and point them in the right direction, to achieve their desired outcome and objective. It is however up to the person to use what you give them, or not. It is not up to you to make them. It is all down to their choices. It is nothing to do with you what they do. You can love that person, give advice to help that person from your compassionate unconditionally loving heart. However, it is not up to you what they choose to do with it. This is where detachment comes in, and the beauty of giving what I will call "space for growth".

"Space for growth" is actually a beautifully assertive space to be in. As it is honouring and loving of the self, and actually of the other person involved. This is simply because you are honouring them enough to step up to the divine level that they so wish to be at. You are supporting them from a distance.

I will take a moment to explain assertiveness here. A number of people confuse it with aggression. This it so definitely is not. It is another word for heartfelt communication. This is a space we must all learn to come from, as it is the space that will bring us closer to the world of our dreams and the life of our dreams individually.

In order to make the changes that we wish to make to each of our individual lives, we must first take charge of our own personal self. We do this by being assertive with both ourselves and the people around us. If something isn't pleasing us then it is perfectly alright to say so. You are being yourself and honouring yourself in heart if you do. What your heart speaks to you, you must follow through to find your happiness and worth, and the life of your dreams. Speak your truth from the heart. As the title of this book says, the answers are always within, if you choose to listen and take that assertive action upon them. When you are assertive and follow your heartfelt guidance through, no matter what it says, even if it seems downright odd at the time, you will always end up better off than you were before, and improve the world around you.

Why?

Well because you have raised the vibration through following your soul's guidance through heartfelt communication. In this space as I have already said, there can be no wrong.

We are souls having human experience, and therefore by default we are naturally happy, joyful and playful beings, that spread love and growth through love throughout the world.

Simply stop taking notice of outside influences, and focus purely and simply on what you desire for you. If something is upsetting to you, say so from an assertive heartfelt viewpoint, that will not offend. Simply say that you are not happy at this time with how things are and that you require space to sort things out for you. If you take this courageous step to be assertive, movement forward can be made in a positive direction. If the other party doesn't take it on board, then that is their choice, nothing to do with you. You do not have to take on their responses. Leave them to it, and simply send them love from a distance.

It is all in the recognition that we are souls having human experience, rather than humans with a soul. This therefore means we are unlimited multidimensional beings that can do anything we choose. We have the ability to make all our desires come true. We simply just need to make it common place to look within to our heart for our answers.

Coming from the heart is an extremely powerful space. It is powerful as it is all loving and all seeing. It is a space where nothing can possibly be wrong. It is also an incredibly playful space, where anything is possible, and magic and miracles can take place.

Have you ever heard the saying "You are only ever as old as you feel". This is a very truthful statement. Also, have you ever noticed that the age you feel in this space is usually when you were young and carefree? I never feel older than 18 years old inside.

Why is this?

Well age is just a number anyway. That is all it is. Unfortunately, many see age as a thing of punishment, and take the "I am another year older, one step closer to death" approach. We humans get things so upside down. It is simply a number of celebration, of how many years we have played at creating dreams in the physical human world. It is another year of wisdom, and heartfelt joyful play, shared with God and all that is. Plus, death has nothing to do with age, one can die at any time.

In truth every night, during the deepest part of our sleep, we are actually dead, off in the Universe picking up titbits to bring back with us. This is why our dreams are so important too. They reveal everything that we need to know about our current position and where we are going, so it is important to take good notes of those dreams that you remember. Write them down, and learn from them, as it is your soul and God telling you about your true self and where you need to be going. I am a very good dream interpreter and have helped a good number get onto their true path of heart by revealing their dreams messages. We actually dream every night, but do not remember them all. They will be recalled to the physical memory at precisely the right time that you require the information. This is why, sometimes, we have deja vu moments. It is simply that we are recalling what we have been told through our dreams.

It is so important to express gratitude for what we experience daily, even waking up each morning. Everything we experience is a blessing that serves us, so be grateful for all that happens to you. As I have told you, when we are dreaming, in the deepest part of our sleep, we are in fact actually dead, and learning from God and the Universe all that we require to know to take us forward in life. So when we wake up in the morning, we have actually come back to life. What a thing to show gratitude for, that our soul has chosen to experience another day playing on Earth through our human bodies. What is there not to be thankful for in that? What a joy it is to open the eyes and witness the dawn of each day, a day that we have created in choosing to come back and play the game of human life to achieve our dreams of heart. WOW. In the wisdom of this do you not feel a shift to joy within you, knowing that every day is a game of creating dreams in reality?

Chapter Five

~

The fact that you choose to wake up and continue to experience human life shows why you are so worthy and deserving of all your dreams to come true for you. You have chosen this human life, to play and see what it is like to achieve dreams in a place of restriction. How funny we souls are to create a game like this. We are simply here to play in the space of all that is, in the "I am" presence.

What is the "I am" presence?

Well, it is the acknowledgement that we are all connected through energy, as we are all the Universe in human form. The Universe, and therefore, all wisdom about all that is lies within us. We are made in the likeness of God, as we are souls, the Universe, Stardust in human form. This is a magical discovery, as it can create miracles for us. It is the realisation that we are unlimited beings, multidimensional, and therefore can see the path of truth for us by going within, taking notice of our dreams, and listening to our intuitive voice of heart, our gut instincts.

We are here to achieve every dream that we have envisioned for ourselves, just the way we want it. To simply live in playful joy and happiness, and follow our hearts desires. You are so worthy and so deserving of all that you desire, and it is what God and the Universe wants for you.

There is one important point to speak on here. It does not happen automatically. It does require action steps from you to make these dreams come to be. You do have to begin to take action on the intuitive thought processes that you have. God cannot give you what you desire, and fill in the "hows" for you, whilst you are busy procrastinating and doing nothing about it. This is why as soon as you get an intuitive heartfelt thought, which makes your heart jump in delight, take action on it instantly. If you allow the human brain to become involved, all that "mind talk" and fear may stop you from taking action. If a heartfelt playful thought comes to you that will take you forward towards a goal, ACT ON IT.

This is also why one should never concentrate on the "How". It is the biggest block in the world to let the human brain become involved in any decision making towards your heartfelt dreams. The answer is to simply flow, listen to the heart and act upon it as you can. God takes care of the "How's". You are simply here to flow, play and enjoy the journey towards your dreams, challenges and all.

Why should I enjoy the challenges? I hear you say

Well, challenges are your important learning. To know everything that you need to achieve your biggest aims in life, you have to know everything and more that will help you to achieve them. For example, you cannot host a healing support group which helps with all forms of trauma, without knowing how trauma affects people in the first place. Our challenges are teachers that will ultimately help us achieve our dreams. Therefore we need to be as thankful, and full of gratitude for our so called challenges, as we are for the hugely positive leaps we make towards our goals and dreams. Challenges are our school, what we learn from, that the heart turns into productive abundant play, in all ways for all of humanity.

This means that we do ultimately have to turn everything on its head. There are some that do this naturally without effort. Have you ever noticed that a successful business owner is always happy, and has a playful way about them? They may not know a thing about working in conjunction with God and the Universe. They just naturally have the ability to achieve precisely what they want. First of all they believe that they are worthy and deserve the business outcome they envision. Also, they take action on every possibility to achieve it that comes into their head. If one comes to a so called "dead end" they sit and listen for the next plan of action that excites the heart, and act on that. They keep following this process until their goal and more is achieved. The truth of the matter is, the outcome of the dream is always much better and magical than ever envisioned. All they have done, purely and simply, is follow their excitable heartfelt feelings with ease and grace, until the desired outcome and beyond. They may know nothing at all about the fact that they are souls having human experience, but they know the joy of what listening to your intuitive guidance of heartfelt feeling can bring you.

In the same token, there are those that have achieved their dreams in the way above, then lost it again, and then found the ability to regain it. What happens in these instances?

The truth of the matter is, in these instances, they have simply allowed the human mind to come in, fears that they may lose the dream they have made their reality. Low and behold it happens that the fear creates the reality of lack, through the law of attraction. The result… they lose what they have created through listening to their "mind talk". However, they have known what it was to manifest and attract precisely what they dream of, so are able to regain what it is they have lost through remembering their old natural skills of following the heart.

This draws me to another important human issue. This is around mental illness. All mental illness shows the astonishing power of human emotion over soul feelings. For example, all people fall somewhere upon the Asperger's scale, so this is where I am going to place my focus. I am aware however, that all mental conditions show a definite split between soul and human. All people that have a mental illness label can indeed have a split personality. They can be all soul, from the heart and extremely pure, innocent and childlike people, which contain immense wisdom. In this space they are completely connected and know instantly the area, usually one specifically, where their soul can shine and give its message to the world. However, put under pressure or in situations slightly out of their soul's purpose, then you see totally human mind and emotion coming from them. They appear fractured from their heart centre, and anger, frustration and all other egotistical emotion comes flooding from them. They throw powerful tantrums, and then their soul cries for the pain expressed and they come back to flow and connection. They show the extremes of all that humanity has to offer and all the soul has to offer in the same person. Basically, the integration of human and soul isn't complete, and they can sometimes fracture into the extremes of each. The truth is though, in connection with their soul they know exactly who they truly are, where they should be and how they are required to put their uniqueness and vibration raising purpose into being. This is what society in general, and indeed governments need to realise, and act upon to assist people to help themselves, and then the world with their wonderful uniqueness and wisdom.

Currently society in general, and governments, through lack of awareness, put pressure where there is no need for it. As people with conditions like Asperger's are able to work, they simply just have the view that they can do anything, and when it suits, put them under unnecessary pressure and remove all assistance. Governments need to realise that they too, are in a position of service to all that they care for in each individual country. They are not there to line their own pockets and play chess with real people's lives and play High School debates, they are there to serve. To realise they are in a position of service to all people, no matter which party they are, will bring a natural shift in focus, and action made accordingly from this new focus will bring positive change in this area. Yes, people with conditions like Asperger's can work, as can all people. As I have already said, every single person is on the spectrum. It is just that those with more specific symptoms need more help to repair and move forward. However, they are always highly intelligent and very wise people, and this needs to be acknowledged. People diagnosed with a mental condition generally have a single area where they shine, whether it be in science, computers, music or any other area, they just require a little more help to get started in that field. Everyone has the right to shine. For sure, each person that is diagnosed knows everything and more about their one area, but are just unsure about starting the steps to get there. Their focus is always on their chosen area, and therefore they are usually magicians in attracting miracles around it. They just have no idea where to start regarding how to attract it into their life, as they can be fractured and not completely integrated to listen to the soul all the time. This is where the lack of insight from people and government keeps putting unnecessary blocks and pressure in the way, instead of aiding their flow by providing someone to fill in the gaps of progress. It is time for governments, and indeed all people, to be truly in service to each other, and see where the help for repair is required specifically. Ultimately, it will help raise the vibration of all people, as mentors are put in place to assist dreams.

Those mildly on the Asperger's scale can simply begin to focus and attract what they need to them now, and seek mentors that will assist them in their quests. Those further on the Asperger's scale require governments to be more understanding and fulfil their mission of service to provide assistance to all routes of occupation. Each person that comes forward knows where they will naturally shine and help the world most, so just provide the route for them to get there. All people deserve and are worthy of having their dreams fulfilled, and know precisely where they need to be to fulfil them. It is time to help all souls to shine, rather than hinder them and fracture people with unnecessary human pressures. This is true for all mental illnesses. It is in this area that humanity can currently have the completely opposite focus to what is required. All people with mental illness are all a genius at something, so simply help them to shine rather than hinder them.

In truth you attract and manifest what you think about the most. The law of attraction, is an incredibly powerful space. Focus on what is wrong, and what you lack in your life, you attract that. Focus on what is right, and the dreams that you wish to create for yourself, and that becomes your reality. The human brain tells you all that is wrong with your life, and your heart tells you all that is right with your life. So ultimately, it is the one that you give the most focus to that ultimately will win out. So choose your choice wisely. All required wisdom is all stored in the heart. In saying that I have told you where to look always for your guidance. The heart is the soul's brain, and ultimately our truthful and most honest brain. It is also the space from which you attract all positive experience, through the law of attraction, which provides yet another reason to give the heart your undivided attention, in regards to where you go and what you do in your life.

You and your experiences in physical life, are what you choose to give the most attention to. Focus on fun, play and creating your dreams through the law of attraction then that will be your experience. Focus on everything that is wrong in your life, and what you don't have… in other words, the lack, you will create more lack, and ultimately move into a life that isn't serving to you or anybody else. So give focus to the positives in every circumstance, even if they are extremely few. Always give the positives the main focus of your attention. Even if there is only one thing to be happy about, give that the focus of your attention, as it will attract more to be happy about and give thanks for through the law of attraction.

Chapter Six

As I have told, we are in the process of switching to new ways of being. The ways of listening to the brain, and functioning through agenda is no longer going to work for us. Give the brain power and you will create more that you do not wish to experience.

We are as a collective being taught to switch to the heart to create positive experiences for ourselves, even out of situations that are considered to be "negative". Let's look for a moment at the big issue of the time, terrorism.

In truth this situation can only exist in our world if we give it the power to be there through our fear, anger and other egotistical emotions. Terrorists are purely and simply our fears put in front of us in form. As I said earlier, the news and press do nothing to lesson these fears in people. I ask you from the centre of my heart to stop watching the news and buying newspapers. All they do is empower your physical brain to be fearful, and therefore they bring more to be afraid of into your life. To alter this view upon terrorism, we need to switch the situation onto its head.

They are thinking that they are causing fear and taking over the world by using violence. Turned on its head though, look really at what they have done. All countries have joined together as a strong community. We have faith in each other that we can overcome the threat of terrorism, and we are joining together to do so. Ultimately they are doing the opposite to what they think they are achieving. In our heart space we are unified in friendship against a fear monger. That is a very powerful space to be in, and can achieve miracles for the world. Giving focus to the unification and togetherness they have created, allows us to focus on a more loving perspective, rather than a fearful one. The world as we know it, isn't being destroyed by these people, it is actually being healed through the unification and belief that we can overcome it. We are doing the best we can with what we have.

I do not necessarily agree that fighting fire with fire, by using warfare, is the best approach to overcoming terrorism. What I do believe is that each government is doing the best it can, with the knowledge that it has, to protect its people. Where there is positivity of heart to achieve something, the ways and means of achieving it will always be improved upon as the relevant people become wiser, through learning the use of loving heart and the law of attraction. We are learning a lot about how to be positive in the face of adversity, during this period of time.

The "real" ways to overcome any so called threatening behaviour, is found through wisdom in the heart space. There is a difference between wisdom and knowledge. Wisdom, is what we already know deep within us. It is the source of what we are. We access our wisdom through our heart space, and acting on our gut instincts without hesitation. Knowledge on the other hand is something that we learn, and is often stored in the physical brain. Knowledge is where we humans can put ourselves in boxes, and can become what I call "grey people" or "text book people". Answers always come from doing something "outside the box". Knowledge is there to assist and fill in things we may have forgotten, but a solution is always found by looking beyond knowledge and doing something inspired that is a little bit different. It is often the "eccentrics" of the world that come up with the best solutions to problems, as they will never allow themselves to be trapped by what is in a textbook. All inventions and insight comes from people that dare to be different, and see there can always be something more than what is currently available, or in front of them to solve an issue. If the wise eccentric did not exist, we would still be in the dark ages, without cars or computers, or anything else that has brought humanity forward to its current state of being.

To solve any issue that arises for us therefore, we must drop this, "We have learned this, so it must be so" approach. It is no longer the way to be. It is the way that has got us "lost in our direction" after all. To achieve results that will truly work against such things as terrorism, we need to look beyond what we have learned, into what we know through our wisdom of soul. Dare to be the loving playful eccentric to see and create the true solution to any issue. It is those people that are classed as eccentric or quirky, that contain the ability, to be wise, and look beyond what we are taught through textbooks. We have lost the ability in recent years to use our natural wisdom within, and have got to a space of being totally reliant upon the textbook answers, to achieve any solution. It is time to move on from this approach, as it has not worked for us. It is time once again for the divine loving happy go lucky eccentrics to step forward again, and provide the solutions.

The divine eccentrics of old, that provided all our wonderful solutions of the past problems experienced, are beginning to disappear from the world, transform, and go to other dimensions. They are leaving space so the wise, eccentric fun people of the new ways can step up and show the world how to repair and move forward from this space of fear and stagnation. If you are reading this book, I am pretty certain that you are one of those very people I am speaking of. Eccentrics have been forced into hiding in recent years, through misunderstanding of the "textbook" people. It is absolutely time for you to come out and shine wherever you are. Make yourselves known, as you provide the wise solutions of the future. It is time for the eccentric daredevils to "Step up" and "step out" into the world, and bring it back into the loving peaceful balance we have lost.

Chapter Seven

There is one thing that I am very aware of in our current worldwide climate, and that is that many of humanity are closed to hearing intuitive guidance, and rely on our physical mind to take us forward. So what can be done to change this?

The breath, as I have said before, is a very powerful natural gift that we possess, that can, used effectively, take us straight into our heart space, and therefore the truth of all that is. A golden tip for you. As soon as a "negative" thought comes into the brain, before it even takes hold, take a deep breath into the abdomen, and see yourself breathing out the thought and all that is connected to it. Actually do this with all "mind talk", and you will be connected to your worth, value and dreams before you know it.

Avoid all things that activate your physical mind to fear, so you can take more time to experience the joy that is around you, and the pleasures that the Universe can give you through the heart.

In truth, the art of using the breath to remove all thoughts that are disserving, is a skill that requires mastery. As humans we have fallen into the space of believing we are humans with a soul, and have got into the pattern of taking more notice of the brain instead of the heart. We are as a collective waking up to the wisdom of the heart space, and working with God to achieve our goals and objectives. Through realising we are worthy of our dreams, going into the heart space to hear the route to achieving them, will become second nature.

Having said that, there is no one, no matter how in the heart space we are, that doesn't experience thoughts of ego, when we are flowing towards our dreams. The difference with those who achieve the dream, is that they carry on regardless. They know that it is part of the journey to the dream envisioned, so push through the "fear blockades" that the human brain puts there and still achieve the aim.

It is all about being in your heart, and shining out from a loving space. In the new space we are moving into, there is no such thing as right or wrong. There is no such thing as karma either. We are all precisely where we need to be at any given moment. Everything is working out precisely as it needs to in perfect divine timing. In truth, what you desire already exists for you in another dimension, and you are simply moving us forward in consciousness by manifesting it in the present moment. The more compassionate and unconditionally loving you are, the more you attract to you, with speed, on your journey. Miracles happen in that playful heartfelt space, through the realisation that we are souls having human experience. Feel the expansion and growth in your heart in the realisation of that.

All is play if you listen to your heart. It is interesting to note, that the things you most fear, and keep away from if you listen to your "mind talk", are the skills, and things that you require to achieve the dreams, and help humanity to move to a better space of consciousness. Be mindful of this fact. For example, I have always had an issue with public speaking when in the physical mind. Of course, as I write this, and through my connection to my heart space, I know that I need to push through this issue, to come and speak to you in more depth about what is written in these pages. So again, write down everything that comes up for you. What are your greatest fears? What are your greatest joys? The answers to these questions, can tell you so much about your soul's purpose here, and what you should be doing to help humanity move forward towards the "dream world" we envision and talk about.

Never underestimate the power of visualisation, and behaving as though you have the dream in your life already. This is a sure way to manifest it to you even faster.

Feel it, believe it, know you are worthy and deserving of it, and purely and simply BE IT.

It is in a way like being an actress on stage. You behave and act as though that is your life. The outcome through the playfulness of that, is the reality of your dreams in form. What could be better than that? It is all about play.

This is why I love being around children and animals. They haven't lost their connection to where we come from and the fact we are stardust, and part of the Universe in form. They are so playful and so full of energy through this connection. Yes they need to learn boundaries, we all do, but ultimately through spending time around children and/or animals, we learn how to play in the world, and create what we desire for ourselves through simply loving one another and playing until what we desire is delivered to us. The only reason that we "grown-ups" tend to lose this is because we have held on to experiences that haven't necessarily been positively serving to us and held onto what we have been told unpleasantly by others. We have allowed ourselves to be taken from, and lose the wisdom we naturally have as children to attract things to us. Through spending time with them in playful abandon, we can regain this ability to

29

naturally attract exactly what we want when we want before we even ask for or about it. WOW, what a blessing they are to us. Give gratitude for them, and every experience that you have with them. They are teaching you to reconnect with your truth and who you truly are.

Chapter Eight

Being in the present moment is another thing that attracts what we desire to us much quicker. After all, the past has already been, and the future is yet to be, so what is the point of dwelling or worrying about either. There is absolutely no valuable reason for either of these things. Worrying is a pointless emotion, it really doesn't serve any form of valuable purpose, either does dwelling on the past. If anything they block your progress, as they keep you in a space that isn't serving to you or anybody else around you. The present moment on the other hand is immensely powerful.

What you do in any given moment, creates your future, so make every moment count, and be positively productive for you. Never feel that you have to fill every moment with noise and doing. Silence and peaceful nothingness are good spaces. If nothing is there in a moment, simply enjoy the peaceful silence. Better that, than draw something to you that isn't serving by making it a moment of worry instead. There is nothing to be afraid of in silence. Silence is powerful, as it attracts more peace into your life, rather than hardship. Make every moment serve you, and add to your adventure on Earth. As long as you are in flow with your heart and acting on your gut instincts you can do no wrong. All is as it should be for you, so if a moment pops up that only contains peaceful silence, enjoy that as much as the moments of motion. Silence is where inspiration comes in, there is absolutely nothing wrong in it. It is as productive as the moments of bustle. All is good and all is serving you, so enjoy the present no matter how it arrives or what it contains, simply just BE in the NOW.

This state of BEING in the moment, I refer to as "Buddha time". When we really are just in presence, there is absolutely nothing to concern yourself over. You can simply be a happy, loving vessel, doing your part to assist yourself, and all humanity at the same time. Raising your vibration, raises the vibration of everyone else. Therefore, all moments are serving when in presence of the "I am" that you are. The space of the "I am" is all powerful, it confirms that you are the Universe in form, and completely at one and in connection to all that is. Any thoughts, or actions that take you from this space, are teaching you about it. Out of it, can be quite literally mayhem, so to find this joyful peace in the moment, once you have reached it is something that you will never wish to sway from.

If something pops up, or someone says something to take you out of this moment of Joyful loving abandon, simply say thank you for their time and move away from the person. If it is a stressful thought of the past, or the future, that has come into your present acknowledge it and thank it for showing itself to you. In either case, whether it be a thought or a person's statement to you, it's possibly something that you may need to know more about and research in the next moment to take you forward in your life, and create a dream for you. As a result always be thankful for every moment, no matter what it provides for you. It is always serving to you in some way.

The moment of "I am" presence, and complete oneness with everything that exists, is something that we initially have to work at. However, as it is a space that is so joyful and wonderful to be in, we wish to experience it more and more. So achieving it once found is something that soon becomes second nature, purely because it is our natural default state, and we wish to remain in it at all times. It is a space where Karma does not exist. It is a space where there is no right or wrong, everything just simply is as it should be at all times. Therefore, absolutely nothing should be allowed to take you from this magical, miraculous space.

There is a little issue that arises out of the human acknowledging they are a spiritual being. They realise that they are spiritual, but they continue to look to outside reasons for how things are for them. Quite often, more than I would care to mention really, spiritual people have got into the habit of blaming "Past lives" for how things are in their present. This is absolutely wrong. Reincarnation does exist, but again it is something that happened in the past, and therefore has no hold over your present. This makes the issue of Karma obsolete. Past lives are as much focusing on something in your past, that isn't serving your present, as a bad experience during your childhood in this life. Simply stop looking to anything in your past, to blame for things going wrong in this life. Any form of past focus isn't serving. It is in fact blocking your movement forward towards your dreams. Anything that comes up from the past, whether it be in this life or a past life, can be acknowledged and released from you in the moment it arises. By all means acknowledge that it has come up, and indeed if you wish write down what it has brought up for you, so that you can, learn from it, and move forward from its lesson. However, do not dwell or spend days focusing on it, as it isn't serving to you, or anybody

33

else to do so. Leave all aspects of the past where they are meant to be, in the past. They have been and gone, and therefore have absolutely no hold whatsoever on your present. What you do in each present moment, is what counts and what can be life changing for both you and the world. Stay in your point of power. The point of power is the present moment. Feel its peace and its joy, as it takes you forward in magical ways to fulfil your dreams.

Chapter Nine

Writing about the power of the present moment, has inspired me to discuss what makes you aware that you are out of connection with yourself and the "I am" presence. One of the ways of knowing you are out of tune with yourself is tiredness. Tiredness shows that you are out of sync with your truth, and also possibly are doing too much for others, and not giving yourself enough care. It shows that you are not quite in that childlike innocent playful space of the present moment, that brings you endless energy and good health. In the new space, of continuous presence of moment, we are moving into, less is more. Focusing on loving and healing the self comes first before the care and repair of others.

The "Less is more" philosophy, is all about BEING in the moment. It isn't about how much "stuff" you can fit into the next hour, or whether you can get a list as long as your arm completed in a day. Have you ever noticed, on days where you try to fit everything in at once, you are always incredibly tired? This is because it has "taken you out of yourself". You are usually nowhere near being in the present, as you are worrying about finishing your list in the time allocated in a day. How can you be of use to anyone else, if you are stressing about what you have to do? In truth you simply can't. So whenever you are experiencing any form of tiredness, or indeed ill health, stop and take the time for you. It is absolutely essential to take time for yourself to replenish. It is all about honouring and loving yourself. The world will not end because you have taken time to honour you and all that you are, and simply BE in peace in every moment. Taking this time for you is serving, and therefore serving to everybody else too, and it will without a doubt bring swifter positive changes in the world. You cannot do anything in the service of humanity and change the space of the world in a positive way, without taking the time to focus on healing and loving the self, in each present moment.

In all honesty, how can you expect others to love you, and respect you unconditionally, if you are not doing those things for yourself first? It is an absolutely crucial element of creating the life you envision and desire for yourself. In taking the steps to care for the self in all ways, you are ultimately shifting the denseness that humanity has come to know. It is only through positive, loving and compassionate care of the self, that the "dream world" we envision will come to be for us.

One can only realistically focus on one's own space. The truth of the matter is, that is actually the only space that we really have any form of control over. Many make the mistake of trying to control others, and try to make others their version of them, to make this happen. Again it is a circumstance where human nature has got things back to front. This has got to stop. Focus on you and you alone. When you focus purely and simply on yourself in the present moment, there are no problems at all to contend with, and all is well. Clear out all the garbage you have taken on from others, and old patterns that you have taken on without realising as you were growing up. Everything we are as a human we learn to be from others. In the same way they can be removed, simply by following our gut instincts and feelings of heart, in each present moment as it arrives, whether it be a moment of peace, or an impulse to action. It is all about being in the moment, and pushing through all that isn't serving to us regardless.

Accidentally taking things on from other people, in regards to behaviour and reactions to circumstances, is actually something that is very easy for us to do. From the moment we are born in human form we are like sponges that soak up everything. There is no blame for any aspect of this, it just simply happens. It is a DNA imprint, which creates this situation for us, and also the fact that our soul has an antenna which can easily attract such things to it. In the space of self-love and care, we can remove all the "muck" we have collected without even knowing it. It is the breath that can aid you in this, along with positive affirmation. The breath is a very powerful tool that we naturally have in our possession. Any negative thoughts or emotions come through, take a deep breath into your abdomen, see them leaving you as you breathe out and then affirm something along the lines of, "I am loved and loveable. I am worthy, I am deserving of everything that I desire, and it flows to me with divine ease and grace".

Patience is required for this activity, as many things may come up for you. From experience, patience isn't always a human strong point. The physical human body has the ability, to pull you away from those things that will assist you the most. This is where mentors, like myself, and many others come in to help you in many ways. We help you to push through the barrier of impatience and fear of change, to achieve your dreams and objectives.

If you are ready for the change to come into your life, you will make it happen for you. What you envision and see for you, and believe in, can be the only outcome for you. What you choose to focus on the most in your life, is what you bring in for you, whether it be positive or negative.

If you are ready to bring in change, listen to your intuitive guidance, and follow it. You will have been guided to buy this book for example. Perhaps, in the future, you will be drawn to another book or a course that will assist you in your growth. Follow every positive impulse that comes to you, as in truth it will bring you closer to the true soul being that you are, and the direction that you have always envisioned for yourself. There can be no wrong in your choices. Whatever the outcome of it is, it is right for you. Whether it appears to be good or bad, it is correct, as everything, and I mean everything, which you experience is taking you closer to your worth, and your hearts desires, all the time. Be grateful for every experience, whether it teaches you about the denseness of humanity, or the freedom of your soul, and your truth for you. Whatever the experience, it is all good, and always perfectly timed. Simply follow your heart and gut reactions always, as they will bring you to your desired results.

Chapter Ten

When I referred to the "new space" that we are moving into earlier, many may have drawn the conclusion that I mean everyone has to be "spiritual". It doesn't mean, in any way, that everyone in it is spiritual, in the way that the term is currently meant. The term "spiritual" currently has an air of being separate from all other people. There is actually no separation among any living creature, as we are all energetically connected and from the same source, whether we be human or animal. Therefore, no matter what background you come from on a physical level, whether you know it or not, we are all spiritual beings, on a mission of service for all humanity. In acknowledging and accepting the wisdom in this, it means that everyone, every single person in this world, is moving into a pure heartfelt space, and divine heartfelt flow and shining out their truth for all to see.

Wherever we are in the transitional phase from being completely human, to being spiritual beings of soul, we will always require teachers, lawyers, builders, musicians, in fact every profession that currently exists, in our new way of being. All that will be different is that all will be where they choose to be and dream of being, and not just going along with the "humdrum", thinking they are doing the right thing in pleasing people. People pleasing is becoming a no. It is yet another area where we have got used to doing things back to front in the physical human space. People pleasing actually means giving your power away to another, because you are doing what they want you to do, rather than following your heart. The new way of being is all about loving the self, and self-care. As I said before, it is a space where less is more. Even empathy becomes a thing of the past in this space. Self-empowerment will come in and become a thing of the norm. Many make the mistake in thinking that a lack of empathy and people pleasing will make the world a cold place. I tell you now, it will not. It will empower it. The reason for this I have said earlier. If you begin to focus on each given moment that exists for you, it will only exist for you. Yes other people may be experiencing their own "moments in time" in close proximity to you, and may even give the appearance of sharing it with you. However, each moment in time is in fact just yours, and therefore is a very pure innocent and joyful heartfelt space. It will bring an end to all the "negative" emotions that currently exist, and make every moment one of pure love. In actual fact, therefore, there will be more love in the world than there is now, in every single way. Love is the only feeling that will have any presence. This is because in reality it is the only truthful honest feeling that exists. All others come from outside influences. In a pure moment of presence all that exists is love, peace and harmony. What a wonderful realisation.

Because empathy and people pleasing are coming out of the equation, there must be remembrance that we are only in charge of ourselves. We can only ever be responsible for ourselves and what is happening in our own space and life. It is through taking charge of ourselves and our own personal lives that we aid growth and transformation in the world.

Those, like myself, that are there to assist in the repair of others on their journeys, MUST take responsibility for our own self-care and growth, and work together as a team to achieve the required goal... the repair of humanity. Collectively, we also must concentrate on clearing ourselves towards the "pristine vessel", and also work collectively together towards the goal we envision. We are separate yet together in the goal of transformation and positive growth to love and shining. These actions of clearing out all that isn't serving us, ultimately will bring us to the repair of humanity.

Those who are the healers and carers, in divine service to all humanity, please remember your self-care. Healing cannot fully take place in another, whilst you are carrying "muck" in yourself. When you see it written like this, it appears to be rather obvious, and yet, many are "out there" giving what they refer to as "healing" when they are still carrying issues in themselves. Please stop. Remember less is more. If you are in a space where you are in high stress, take time out for yourself. You cannot heal in this space, and actually are in danger of transferring your stuff to the person that has come to you for help. This isn't healing for anybody. In times of dis-ease and stress, simply and gracefully take the time to heal yourself. All is well and working in perfect divine timing for you. Just purely and simply believe it. All is, always, perfectly well and as it should be. This is true for all people in all walks of life and occupations, and is very important to achieving personal happiness and the human life that you want for yourself. We are all equal, no one is above or below another, and we are all practicing in our own divine spaces, in whichever field we choose to be in.

As humans we have, to a certain extent, lost our way, and have fallen into the trap of being "workaholics". Oh dear... poor people. Less is more. You cannot do your profession, whatever that is, when you are exhausted from doing too much of it. No one will benefit from this. Neither you, nor the people you are trying to assist. Again, I say to you please stop, step back, and take time for you to grow and repair. When you have taken this "time out", to heal and look at where you are, and what you want for yourself, then you can come back to it with a completely different outlook. A more free and happy outlook will bring positivity, and indeed be more productive for all in the situation.

Some people, however, work in a situation where things are piled on top of you from other people, like a counsellor, psychologist, or any other healing, caring profession, where you are clearly in service to another. You can, in these professions of care, accidentally at times take things on board from your clients, that are not yours, and therefore do not in any way belong to you. Certain aspects of the situations you have heard, have struck a strong chord with you, and you accidentally hold onto them, and keep thinking about them. This is all ok. Whatever is happening is for your growth, so acknowledge what it is saying about you. The reason that you have held onto it, is because it touches an aspect of something within you that isn't yet cleared. They are actually mirroring something in you, in these situations. Everything is all about you, and what is clearing and going on within you, so take good notice of it. Some in these situations will naturally take the very human response and seek out other people to talk to, rather than deal with it themselves. This is not necessarily the best angle to take. This is because if you find someone to talk to, you are simply spreading the issue around, passing it onto someone else, and giving it more power to exist, rather than clearing it away. In order for everyone to stay powerful and in their own personal space, in situations such as this, you must find a way to clear it on your own, or at least appearing to be alone. The truth is we are never alone, as energetically we are all connected and part of the Universe. The answer in these situations is to write everything down, as a letter to the Universe or God. Include in it all your thoughts and feelings around what happened, and then simply destroy it in any way that is good for you. This can include burning it, or simply tearing it up and throwing it away. In doing this, you are in fact removing the situation from you, so it can never return. You can take this action around any issue or situation that arises for you to clear it from the body for good.

You are at all times exactly what you choose to think about yourself and what is going on around you. So purely and simply if you do not like what is going on for you, change your focus to what you wish to bring in and experience. The more you focus on what you want in your life, the more that will become your experience. Pure and simple.

Everyone, at any given time is always a reflection of what they are thinking and choosing to believe in about themselves, and what is going on around them. This is why being precisely in the moment can be so magical. In the space of the moment, you are exactly where you dream of being without having to do anything at all. You naturally believe in yourself, love and value everything about you and where you are. After all in the moment, there is nothing else, as a moment isn't long enough to find any form of issue, so all there is in it is perfection. This is why in a pure loving moment, you have total honour and respect for yourself, and therefore everyone and everything around you. The magic and miracles begin to unfold in your life, when you find and work with this space constantly. You can be and do anything in this space, and you are, as there is nothing else in that moment other than what you choose to believe is true for you.

Those with the easiest lives, by appearance, can often actually have experienced the hardest and toughest of experiences. The only difference is that they have always pushed on regardless with a smile on their face, and achieved their dream. They have remained in the moment and the pure, loving, honouring respect of it, and still seen the dream being real in spite of any hardship that has tried to divert them from it. The present moment is so incredibly powerful and creating for you.

This draws me to bring up illness and dis-ease in the body. In this modern "workaholic" environment, it is becoming much more prevalent, than it ever used to be. People are sometimes being forced to retire early due to stress related illness. As part of the equation, and self-worth, you need to begin to listen to your body's messages. When you are getting aches and pains, don't just take a pain killer and carry on. Instead, stop and acknowledge it, give it thanks for showing you that you are doing too much, and take the time to rest, and repair. Any ailment that shows itself to you is a reflection of your lifestyle and the environment that you live and work in.

The environment that you live and work in, is possibly the only outside thing that has effect on you and your way of being. For example if your environment is damp it will affect your joints and possibly your chest. So if you are prone to aches and pains, observe your environment and if it is damp, do something about it. Also, many allergies are started by a dusty environment, and also if you are an untidy person, and hoard stuff, you are more likely to be stressed than if you take the minimalist approach.

Some people have a little pet hate regarding cleaning and tidying up. This is where that will begin to change if you take good notice. As I said your environment is a reflection of you, so the dirtier your environment, the more things your body holds that are not serving to you. In taking the time to sort out your home and/or workplace environment, giving everything a place and cleaning and dusting it, you are actually cleaning out yourself. Cleaning and tidying maybe a thing that you put off, but when you have spent the time to do it, have you ever noticed you feel better within the self and have a spurt of more positive flow in your life? Even things that can be considered a chore can be beneficial.

This is also why it is important to have your own space, within a home or workplace. Unless you live or work on your own, the environment is shared and therefore a reflection of everyone who lives in it. Therefore, always make sure that you have your own personal space within an environment, which you can be in charge of, and make a reflection of how you are, without being influenced by anyone else. If your personal environment is clean and tidy, then so is your vessel, if it is a mess, it is time to take some space for yourself, and clean up and clear out all that isn't serving from your environment and yourself. As one enhances the other, working on both at the same time will work magic for you, in moving forward towards your dreams and improving physical health on all levels.

Make sure you take time to clear out your environment and yourself, during some part of everyday. You do not need to hoard, or hold onto stuff that isn't serving to you, or providing any purpose. Clear out on all levels so you can move forward to a fulfilled and happy life. Always take the time to make every area of your life and yourself pristine, so that you can be fully, deeply and completely fulfilled in all areas of your life.

If you find it difficult at first to see a starting point for you, know that it is absolutely ok on every level to seek assistance. There are people in all areas of service, waiting to help you achieve what you want in your life. Feel able to call on them. We are all here to help and assist each other to grow. I am happy to assist anyone who turns to me for help, near or far. With the wonderful invention of the internet, it is possible to help people all over the world, without leaving the home. All creations exist to assist us in repair. For example, I am an Empowerment and Transcendence Coach, Assertiveness Coach, Healer and Clairgnostic. All that I do can be done in person or apart, by making use of the web, even the healing and readings. This is possible because of the energetic connection all of humanity shares with one another. We all come from the same source. Every time a star dies, all that is required to create a human or animal is released, and a person or animal is born somewhere. We are all the Universe in form. Even though we are all connected in this way, we also have our own separate space and purpose in the world. We are souls experiencing human existence, and therefore multidimensional. This means we can be in one space, for example our home and work environments, and also, across the world in another space all at the same time. We are everywhere. This is the true reality. It is the realisation of this and therefore the connection in this space, which allows for things like distant healing and readings to take place. It is also the space when we truly find it where we can experience true joy. It brings the realisation that we are never alone, even if we are by appearance. It also brings the wonderful wisdom that everything is an illusion, and completely created by us. We are our own ship's Captain. No one is in charge of, or in any way has the right to control, or tell us what to do. What we choose to think about and give focus too becomes our reality. If we focus on "negative" things, we have "negative" experience. In the same token someone who thinks "positively" will have "positive" experience. You are what you think about, so choose your thoughts wisely.

All those who are wanting a change of life because you are working too hard, know that you can absolutely, under no uncertain terms achieve it. Simply step back and take time out, sit in your own space, breathe deeply in and out, and listen to any intuitive feelings that you have in regards to changing your direction, or how things are going for you. Acknowledge all that comes to you in this space, whether it is things to release and remove from you, so you can move forward, or whether it is simply joyous thoughts to show you your direction. Deeply and completely acknowledge all that comes up for you, and if you haven't a good memory, write it down so you can go back to it at a later date.

Chapter Eleven

⁓

Everything that comes to you in a space of quiet contemplation must be taken notice of, as it ultimately can only serve you to do so. This applies to all people, in all walks of life, and in all occupations. The way to find your answers, and the way of life that you want, is to value your worth, and take time for yourself to discover the path to your dreams, the "how's" that God has there waiting for you to tap into.

You may have many things come forward for you... WOW... if so. This only means that you have many things to teach humanity about themselves. Here, I say powerfully, that you cannot help others effectively, without taking time for yourself. Listen to your body, anything other than feeling bounding childlike energy and joy, carefree and pain free, stop, listen and take good notice of what your body is saying before you go back into the foray. If ever you are feeling anything other than joy about your life, take time for contemplation to discover the intuitive answer to the question that has arisen. There will always be what we call "challenges" that come up for us. They simply exist, as I have said before, to teach us what we need to know to fulfil our dreams, and therefore in the end can and will only be seen as positives. Through, sitting quietly, and going within, answers to every question can be found. It is all about following our intuition.

As humans we can be great "Nit-pickers". Always looking outward for things to complain about and correct. It is something I find very amusing to listen to if I am completely honest. Those who see fault outwardly, have things within them that need repair. The more we focus on self-repair, the less there is to nit-pick about, as we become love in form. Where there is love, and nothing but love, there can be no fear, anger, judgement or any other egotistical emotion. Whilst, we are in a space of transition from one space to another, the "old ways" to the new, there will always be things to clear, as we pick stuff up from those around us, without even realising it. However, if we are also in a space of consciously working towards our dreams, clearing out what isn't serving us, through breath or other means, then we will pick up others stuff less and less, and move closer and closer to what I call the "Buddha state".

At this point, I wish to bring up another issue that has led to our "workaholic" current state of play. It has generally come into existence through our thought and belief patterns about money. This again has come to be through the thought patterns that we have around it, this ancient belief that we have to "work hard for a living". This is a viewpoint that needs switching on its head. I ask you to remember "Less is more". I can hear the statements from you to this "I can't possibly work less than this and have a life and care for my family"... Let me ask you this... If you are a "workaholic", are you spending time "having a life", or being with your family? I think I can deduce from the fact that you are working hard that the answer to that is no. To change the situation to one that is more serving for you, you first need to realise that money is energy. In that wisdom, you will know that the amount you have at any given time, is in ratio to how much you feel that you deserve. If you are in flow and feel your worth and value in having the life you dream of, what you spend comes back to you multiplied. It all comes down to your perspective.

There are some very wealthy people in this world. They have achieved that wealth because they believe they deserve it. They also see life as play and therefore have attracted everything they have dreamed of. The way to stay stagnant, in a life that isn't serving for you or anybody else, is to take it seriously. Taking anything seriously, is one of the biggest blockers in existence. We are meant to be having fun and enjoying ourselves. The ultimate goal of course, to "play" for a living doing something we love and dream of doing. We are not here to do "work" and take a serious approach. Many of you will be reading this, because you wish to change your life, do something that will bring you joy and abundance, in all areas of it, and ultimately be very satisfying in all ways. I am here to say that everything you desire is absolutely achievable and most importantly YOU CAN DO IT!

You can begin now. Focus on your dream job, life, goals, and write them down or say them out loud to the Universe or God. They know what you are here to do, and are simply waiting for you to take just one small step towards your dream, so they can begin to unfold the magic and miracles that heartfelt joy can bring. Yes, initially you may need to start working the dream alongside that which has stopped bringing you happiness. That is perfectly fine. But what will be magical, is that it will give you a more joyous perspective around that which you are trying to move away from. This will actually amplify the joy of what you are bringing in and therefore attract it to you quicker.

Why does this happen?

It happens because you are in the divine flow of the heart, and you are making your dreams a reality. This means that what you are beginning to move away from, is now funding the creation of a dream. Suddenly there is gratitude for it. Immediately your vibration is raised and so are your energy levels, as you move towards your envisioned dream life. Relationships at work and at home will improve, and guess what your money will by miraculous design begin to increase. It is all about following your hearts desires. There can absolutely be no wrong when you do this. You are raising the vibration for the whole of humanity in doing it, so do it with gusto.

Chapter Twelve

Another golden trick, to bring you to your divine flow of positive attraction is to laugh and see the humour in everything. Even when someone is putting their stress onto you, laugh it off, it is not yours, and actually probably isn't even theirs either. People choose to complain about outside things rather than themselves. In their own personal "I am" space, there is never anything to complain about. People complain about what they observe outside of themselves. It's all ok, everything is, but we need to learn to stop, and simply just focus upon ourselves. When people try and put their "stuff" onto us, pull away, no matter who it is, and give them space to clear and grow above what it is they were complaining over. Nothing is any of your business except yourself, so you are perfectly entitled to pull away and allow them space to grow and shine in their own way. We are not responsible for anybody else's response to situations. So if it doesn't agree with us, we can simply pull away and "detach" from them. This does not make you a cold person, it makes you a person that cares for yourself. That is what we are here to do, purely and simply, care for ourselves first, and help the rest of humanity to grow and repair themselves through example, and what we are intuitively guided to do through our life's purpose.

We can simply be and do anything that we choose. There are no limits to what we can do to help ourselves or others. God is simply waiting for you to take action towards it so he can fill in the "how's", that will take you to the ultimate goal of fulfilling your dreams and more. When there is just you and God in the equation, there can be only magic. You are, and indeed, feel safe, as you know you are working together towards a magical life.

Happiness is the key to a full healthy and happy life, and having a good sense of humour is crucial. If you have the ability to laugh at everything that goes on for you, or that happens in your life, to you and around you, you are well on the way to being abundant and successful in all areas of your life. Seeing the fact that everything is happening precisely as it should, and that you are the conductor of your own experience, gives tremendous ability to laugh and see the humour in all situations.

Laughter is also a wonderful healer. When experiences give the illusion of getting on top of you and creating dis-ease in the body, it is absolutely possible to laugh yourself to health. If indeed you have chosen that to be the outcome of the laughter. Without, having a positive focus on the outcome, you will achieve absolutely nothing. Where there is no positivity, there can be no laughter. It is all about perspective, and how you choose to see things in general. Your focus creates your experience. If you have the ability to laugh in the face of adversity, and see everything that has the appearance of being a "challenge", as a lesson to take you forward to help others, you can bring healing to anything through laughter. You can even bring healing to ailments said to be terminal, like cancer, through laughter. I have the pleasure of knowing a number of people, which have been seriously ill, and refused to take that on board, seeing only perfect health as the result for them. They have in turn achieved that desired result, simply by seeing themselves in full health, at all times, how they feel and behave in that space, and seeing it happening for them NOW, even though at that time they are in a space of illness. This is where I say being in the precise moment, and making it work for you is extremely powerful and can create miracles for you. If in a precise moment you only see yourself in perfect health, how actually can you be anything but perfectly healthy? Thoughts and the belief in the thoughts is so awesomely powerful, it can move mountains in your life. Even if a doctor has told you that you are dying, that is only his view. If you in your space in your precise moment see yourself in perfect health, which thought will win out? Yours of course, as ultimately yours is the only one with any form of power over you in reality. This is why, even when a doctor says you are dying you can turn the situation completely on its head, by having your own personal thoughts and views on your health. You are what you choose to focus on. This is where taking the time to just focus on yourself, without any form of outside influence can bring magic and miracles into your life, and in some cases bring you back to true and full vibrant life.

One of the tricks that people use, when they have seen the magic in having humour, and laughing about any situation or health concern in their life, is simply to shut themselves in a room in front of a TV, watching all their favourite comedies, and laughing heartily at them daily. Whilst laughing at their favourite comedies, they have also held true to holding the vision of themselves in complete health, and having a full and happy life. Through doing this, purely and simply, they have laughed themselves to health, through raising their bodies vibration, to match the vibration of the vision of health that they have in their mind's eye.

I admit this level of mindful concentration to bring about health takes practice. Whilst you hold the belief that health is all there is for you that will be your experience. Even if you require to seek out assistance from the world's many repairers, where there is belief, magic and miracles can and will always happen for you.

You do not have to "buy into" any experience that happens to you or around you. It is through buying into experiences, that we can become stagnant and stuck in situations that are not serving to us. We are souls having a human experience. All is an illusion. We are simply here to experience what it is and feels like to be restricted. The knowledge of that in itself creates humour and therefore laughter. Ultimately, laughter can be used to heal any form of situation or health issue for us, as it immediately takes us back into our heart, the soul's brain, where all can be transformed into positive response. It is also a natural thing that can be propagated from within. As the title of this book says, the answers to all you desire are found within you. You are an AWESOME creation. What a WONDERFUL house your soul has chosen to create for you? Give thanks for your soul's ability to manifest you, to simply play in joyful abandon, to achieve all you have envisioned and dreamed of. WOW. How can one not give thanks for opening their eyes each morning, for another day of play towards your dreams?

Chapter Thirteen

～

We are not here to be what others wish us to be. We lose ourselves by taking notice of outside influence and "buying into" outside situations and influences. Of course, as humans, we are naturally programmed to take notice of them. The physical human exists to provide restrictions for our infinite multidimensional beings to push through, to be in a space of love and wisdom. The human loves the boundary of a "comfort zone", and fears to step outside it. In order to achieve all you have come here to achieve, you must be willing to push your human body into spaces that are uncomfortable for it. Dreams do not happen by staying in "comfort zones". Dreams happen by pushing yourself above and beyond where you ever thought possible. Take any form of step towards a goal and God will fill in the "how's". The end result... well... it will be better and even more AMAZING than you ever thought possible.

To make a dream happen, you sometimes have to put yourself into difficult situations. Sometimes friendships and/or relationships will end and drop away. This is sometimes where we can choose to stop ourselves from pushing forward. We prefer in some ways to stick in spaces that are not serving to us, rather than discover the magic that can come through in pushing for change. Change can be a scary experience for some, as the human brain makes them believe that change may bring worse experiences than staying where they are. This is never the case. Change, no matter what it is will always bring positive results. It is how you transform into the being that you have always envisioned for yourself. Be willing to push for everything that pops up that excites you. It may seem impossible. I assure you, however, it is not. God and the Universe want you to achieve and have everything that you have ever seen for yourself. They cannot assist you though, if you are doing nothing to move towards it. God will not knock on your door and say "here is your dream come true, without you having to do anything for it". That just simply will not happen. You have to act on all your ideas, gut and intuitive feelings of heart. Take one step, and God will turn it into a leap for all humanity. It just takes you to push beyond the "comfort zone" that the human brain has provided for you. Let go of all egotistical responses. Where there is pure heartfelt love there can never be any other feeling. I say feeling, as the soul responds to feelings. Emotions are human, and therefore generally all aspects of the human ego. Love is actually the only pure, truthful, real feeling that exists.

Any form of human emotion other than love, like anger, fear, judgement, jealousy etc. tends to come from a space of misunderstanding of the person or situation. As we grow in the wisdom that we are souls having human experience, there is less and less need for these sorts of emotions. The reason for this is because we can see that there is simply just misunderstanding and therefore sending love to the person and/or situation is the only possible outcome, as we begin to see exactly what is going on.

Another important point to make here is to never take the time to explain your side of any story. For one thing, it shows that you have bought into the situation, and totally taken it on board. But, as well as this, it is a complete waste of your valuable time. Everyone will see a situation as they choose to see it regardless of what you say. Therefore it is a waste of time even beginning to explain your side. Everyone is where they choose to be in their evolvement and that is all. Each person in the situation will have their own view of what happened, and there is no way you will ever change it. Only as they evolve, may they begin to see things in the same way as you. It is all about honouring yourself. Why try and give your energy to someone else? Stand in your power. Accept the situation as it is and let go of it, so you can move forward. There is absolutely no point whatsoever, staying in a situation that isn't serving anybody involved in it.

To let go of a situation, so you can move forward into a more positive and productive space, you can either clear it by writing it in a letter format and destroying it once written, seeing it disappearing from your life as you do so. You can also do it using the breath. Breathe in love and breathe out the situation that isn't serving you, until it has gone from your body and you are back to being your true loving self.

We are by default happy loving beings, without any form of what we choose to call "negative" emotion. So, in any situation that doesn't serve the greater good of yourself and humanity, work on yourself in a loving honourable way until you are back to that loving vessel that you truly are. Seek assistance if you need it, but always take the time, to get back to that loving wise soul that you are. Honour yourself to do that. You are deserving and worthy of it, and it is a true sure way to get you to the life that you envision for you.

Chapter Fourteen

⤳

Did you know that actually 90% of the thoughts, that you have each day are not yours?

Many have no idea of this, but it is the truth. As I said earlier in the book, we are like sponges. If we buy into situations, and other peoples stuff, we make our soul's antenna mucky. The muckier it is the more muck we can pick up from other people. It is through honouring ourselves, and taking the time to clear all that doesn't serve us, that keeps us in our own joyful space.

Detachment and self-care are crucial. You can be loving and still offer that valuable listening ear to another, but you do not have to get involved in what they are telling you. Simply listen, and provide a solution if you see it from your loving space of heart, but never allow yourself to get pulled into the situation in any way. Sit back and look upon it from the space of a loving observer. You will be able to provide better advice, if it is required from this space. Also, because you haven't allowed yourself to be involved in it, you will naturally help the person to raise their own vibration much quicker, and move out of the situation themselves much quicker. Detachment is an incredibly powerful space, that without any seeming effort, naturally raises the vibration of all those around you. This ultimately will bring us to the "dream world" we envision for ourselves much quicker. Getting involved in any situation actually lowers the vibration of all those involved in it. This is not a space that serves anybody. Staying detached and in your power as people turn to you for advice, naturally takes the energy of those involved to a higher vibration, and therefore a space that is serving to all. We are all here in a space of service to one another, and ultimately every single person that exists is a teacher of something. Be brave enough always, to stand in your power, and raise the vibration of those around you. You learn much from being the detached observer, and in this space, you can move forward to be a great teacher. It is all about you and where precisely you are at in any given moment. Always be yourself, it is an incredibly powerful way to be.

Empathy however is removed, when you become detached. This may not be taken favourably initially, as if you are a caring loving person, it will have been a natural stance for you to take in situations, where people have come to you for advice. It is though, a way of becoming involved in a situation, and can therefore lower vibration, and make it take longer to rise above, and step out of any situation that is provided. Loving, powerful, honourable detachment is the way forward, to assist others and raise the vibration quicker. It will ultimately move people forward at a much quicker pace, and create world repair at a magical pace.

Detachment will bring an end to "victim" behaviour. Many love to "play the victim" and gain a sympathy vote, by complaining about all that is going on outside of themselves, and yet not taking one single step to do anything about changing it. What good is there in that? How is it serving anyone? The truth is, it just simply isn't serving anyone at all. If someone around you is enjoying "playing the victim", leave them to it. It isn't your space to get involved in, so simply step back and let them get on with it. It is simply a form of "attention seeking". It isn't serving to them or you to be in that space. Simply move away. As soon as people begin to move away, and the victims aren't getting people to give attention to them, they will begin to step up out of it into a more positive space for them and you. When they have done this to a satisfactory level, then you can gladly accept them again, and move forward together in a more positive way. It is ALL absolutely about listening to yourself, and lovingly honouring all your responses of heart.

All is achievable to the way you want it, by listening and following your inner responses, and positively affirming all that you desire to manifest into your life. Remember you can do anything that you choose to believe and follow through with through positive thought patterns. Statements like "I am worthy", "I can attract to me all that I require for my perfect life before I even ask", are so powerful in assisting you to achieve your dreams, so use them. Initially, it may be a task that requires effort, especially if you have been a person that gets involved in "stuff". But once you start doing it consciously, there will become a time when it becomes a natural thing to think positive thoughts all the time. You are what you think and choose to focus on the most. If you focus and think negatively, you will attract more negative experiences. If you focus and think positively, you will attract more positive experiences. It is all about you.

Self-love is also essential in the mix. Say "I love you" to yourself in the mirror every time you see your reflection. Look directly in your eye as you do so. The first time you do this may be extremely uncomfortable and even painful. You may even be saying the opposite of your current emotion about yourself. Write down what happens to you, and what you feel and go through as you do it, positives and negatives on separate sheets of paper. This is so you can hold on to the positives to empower yourself with, and destroy the negatives, with the intention that they have left you forever. To begin with this exercise may take time, as a lot may come up for you. As your heart begins to open, and you begin to reconnect with the soul and your true journey, it will take less time, and more happiness will begin to flow into your life, and more to be happy about will begin to flow in too.

Happiness is the key to everything flowing as it should in your life, so take the time to do what works for you to bring it in.

Chapter Fifteen

In this joyful space of playful loving self-honouring detachment, there comes the realisation that there is no blame in any situation that arises for us. Blame comes when we look outside ourselves to provide answers for any given situation. As we have already discussed, the answers are found within. Take responsibility for your part in anything that arises for you. You got yourself into the situation, so look inside yourself for the answers to getting yourself out of it. All the techniques that I have mentioned previously, writing down what comes up for you, breathing out the negatives, and affirming the positivity you wish to bring in, are ways to clear from you, what may have been your part in the arisen situation. The truthful fact of the situation is, you are only ever 20% responsible for any complete situation, the rest is from the other person, and outside Universal influences. As only 20% of any situation is down to individual human input, this means usually 60% is down to things outside the control of anybody. This is why there is no blame. How can anyone or anything ever be blamed, when everyone involved has had an input to its creation? All are responsible for the situation, and all therefore are required to accept responsibility for their input.

When I say that around 60% of any situation is down to Universal influences, they are simply there to get you towards your dreams faster. I will readily admit, it may not feel that way in the situation that has arisen for you. It is why playing tit for tat over things will never provide a solution. In actual fact, once the knowledge of how the Universe works is taken in, any form of tit for tat is utterly ridiculous. Taking responsibility for your part in any situation that arises for you, and taking the time to work with yourself to clear what comes up, is what will provide the solution and a quicker movement forward to better places for all concerned. When situations come up simply sit in your stillness and ask, "What is it that I need to clear from myself, to stop this from happening again?", and see what comes up to either write down and destroy or breathe out of you.

In the understanding that we are only 20% responsible for any situation that arises, we discover that there is no need to sue people, be bitter towards people, or accuse people by putting blame on to them in any way. There is just the loving wisdom that people may be evolving at different speeds. Where once there was a perfect fit, there may no longer be as you have grown into your true selves at different paces. Even though we are all connected to each other energetically, as the Universe in form, we are also, as you already know separate individuals in our own spaces. In the wisdom of this, it is simply common sense to see that evolving and expanding in what we know, will happen at different paces for each individual person, and it is all absolutely ok.

Always remember that everything and everyone is always precisely where they should be at any given moment. Nothing is ever wrong, so just go with the flow. It is the quickest way to find constant peace and joy within, and therefore attract all your desires. To remain stuck and stagnant in a space without any vision of the positives, isn't serving to anyone, and will only block progress, and any route that you are trying to make in a forward motion.

Embrace all change. Change as it initially appears may not appear to be serving in any way. However, the outcome of the change long term is always positive. Progress and movement forwards is always good. Whatever, the change is that arises though, make sure you remain detached and in your space. It isn't your job to become involved in everybody else's stuff, especially if you can do nothing about it. Therefore, if someone comes to you moaning about something, do not get involved in the illusion the other person has created. Simply be honest in a polite and assertive way, for example, "Why are you coming to me with this, I can't do anything about it. Perhaps tell the people who are able to help you, and tell them how you would like it to be." Stay detached and in your own moment in time, it isn't your place to get involved in what you can do nothing about. It isn't serving or helpful to anyone in the situation, and it doesn't move anything forward. Detachment in the moment is so powerful as it keeps you in your space, manifesting what you desire, rather than getting caught up in everyone else's story and losing yourself and your journey. Be assertive, and stand in your power, follow your journey alone, and leave everyone else to theirs.

To go with the flow of change, embrace and accept it, is the fastest way to bring peace, forward motion, and where required solutions to any given "issue". Issues are only there if we allow them to be. As soon as we accept the situation that arises for us, completely as it is, without trying to take control and change it in any way, happiness and forward motion comes into the equation. Never stay in a thought pattern or a space that doesn't make you happy and dance with joy. If something isn't working out right, change it in whatever way is fitting, to where you are happy and flowing again. All those that are successful, have done this. Some many times. Be willing to constantly change aspects of yourself, or your direction as your gut instincts provide for you to do so. You are not here to be another person's version of you, you are here to be yourself. This is a pure and simple fact.

As soon as you take charge of yourself and take your own life in hand, magic and miracles will begin to happen for you as your dreams begin to manifest.

Chapter Sixteen

∽

So how do you change to your dream life of happiness, over going along with the humdrum?

Some of you may be in jobs that no longer serve you, in regards to making you happy and fulfilled. This is all ok. It is just simply time for you to move on.

First of all, many are under the false illusion that you have to "work" for a living. This isn't entirely true. Yes, you have to create income to support your lifestyle, but you are here to play and be happy and fulfilled in every way by what you do. So look at your passions, your hobbies, what you do outside of "work". Which one do you love the most? Which gives you the most excitement? I can pretty much say with certainty, this passion of yours is actually something that you can make into your playful living. Begin to look at ways you can achieve this. This action alone will make you happy, as it suddenly makes your "work" simply a means to begin and start on your dream life. WHOOHOO what could be better than that?

You are not here to be anyone else's version of you. Nor are you here to fulfil anyone else's dreams. You are simply here to be yourself, do what fulfils you, and allow God to fill in the "how's" to achieve it. It is all about you. God and the Universe is within you as much as it is around you in form.

Never put all your eggs in anyone else's basket, nor rely on anyone else to make your dreams happen for you. That is a sure way to block your flow, as you have become reliant on outside influences to achieve your goals. I say again… It is all about you!

People may say to you, "You are meant to be here doing (whatever) with me". "We are planning where you are going to be, and what you are going to do when you come". Do not allow yourself to be led by such comments. That person is relying on you to fulfil their dreams for them. Also, if you fall into it, you are becoming reliant upon them to achieve yours. You are ultimately in both instances creating blocks for each other, as you are looking outside yourself to achieve your goal. Outside influences will never get you to where you wish to be in regards to your dreams. Never put the keys to your happiness in someone else's pocket. It will in the end slap you in the face, rather than get you closer to your goals. The answer to any problem, big or small, is always within you. Your feelings of heart, gut instincts, and listening to the inner guidance you receive in your stillness spaces of meditation, are what will take you forward to the fulfilment of your dreams.

Time for you is crucial to achieving your dreams. Less is always more. As you begin to sit in your space more and more, you will begin to trust yourself and what is coming to you more and more too. Then you will begin acting upon it. Magic and miracles will happen right, left and centre in your life as you flow with your inner voice. This is the case because, you are not relying on anyone but you, and the guidance you receive from yourself and God.

Take good notice of everything that you are offered, and the people that you are guided to meet. Nothing is coincidence. Everything you experience, is a creation of your thoughts, desires and responses. Make everything that happens to you, whether it be positive, or initially appear negative, work in your favour. Everything that happens is there to guide you closer to your dreams, or teach you something that you can use to great effect, to help others, in whatever capacity you choose, on the way there. Therefore, make everything that happens to you work positively for you.

At this point I will bring another point up around making your experiences work for you. If something does change in your life, and it isn't quite as you want it, be mindful of where your focus lies within the changes. For example, you may go on holiday, or own a time share somewhere. You have been there many times, as it suits you, but changes have been made in ownership, which has brought into place things that may not agree with you. Where do you focus to bring around the changes you desire?

If you have read and taken on board what I have written thus far, you will already know the answer to this. You focus on what you like about the changes, praise them, and therefore you attract more positives to come in. If you focus on what you don't like, guess what, you will have more to complain about, and it will end up being nothing like what you want. Always, no matter how few the positives may initially be through change, give them power and space to grow, so that you attract more of what you like, and less of what you don't to come into the situation. This is the solution in all walks of life, no matter what the situations or changes may be that come into your life. You always get more of what you focus on the most. So always focus on what you like.

Chapter Seventeen

∾

The philosophy I mentioned in the last chapter also applies to people in your life. Everyone acknowledges aspects of other people that they like, and others they do not. If you praise the things you like, you will see more of them from the person involved. However, if you are constantly complaining about someone, either to them, or behind their back, again you will receive more to complain about from them. It is all about respect. Of course, once again, this starts from learning to respect yourself. How can you expect anyone else to respect you, if you do not show respect and honour of the self?

You have no control over other people or their responses to you. All you can do is show respect to all people, and if they are in the space of self-respect, you will see it returned to you hundred fold. You reap what you sow. Therefore take responsibility for all aspects of you. You are the only thing in this world that you ever really have any form of control over. Therefore, give yourself what you would expect to receive from others first, and allow it to flow from you to raise the vibration and respect of another. Some automatically contain the ability to respect themselves and therefore naturally attract it from others. The rest of us need to work at it. If you are one of these, know that all is well and as it should be. You are having to learn self-respect and love, simply so that you contain the skills and know the processes to get there. When you have mastered the art of doing it yourself, you will contain the answers to pass onto others, and move even closer to your dream life through it, by allowing them to move forward also. If your vibration is naturally high, as in honouring, respectful and loving, purely by being in the presence of others, you will raise their vibration to yours, and your vibration will raise even more in the process. You will get into a space where you begin to change people's lives, purely by saying "hello" to them.

As humans, we often make the mistake of trying to take control of people and situations, thinking that we can bring around what we desire in all cases by force. Wrong. No one has the right to control or demand anything from another. Even though we are part of a collective, and all are connected to each other by energy, we are also very much individuals, and have our own unique paths, in the space of all that is. So as you respect yourself, and concentrate purely on your growth and love of self, you will automatically raise your own vibration. In doing this you will attract even more respect to you, naturally from others, that will bring you closer to your hearts desires.

This will happen for you because, as you concentrate on yourself and raise your vibration, your naturally raise the vibration of those around you. You can purely by looking at and working on the positive transformation of yourself, help the world to change. We are as a collective all energetically connected, so how can you fail to raise the vibration of the world, by raising your own. It is automatic and goes without saying. You can never ever fail to achieve the desired outcome. God and the Universe are in constant support of you, and want you to succeed in achieving all your dreams. Just keep focusing on the best you that you can be, and see everything magically and miraculously unfold before you.

We are moving into a new way of being. So all the old ways that used to work for you, may no longer be serving you as they did. We are in a way being made to "wake up" and raise our game. We have indeed over the last few years "lost our way" so to speak. We have been shaken up by worldwide experiences, and so called "challenges", have been for most, a thing of the norm. We are beginning to come out the other side. But in order for our desires to be, the things discussed earlier about concentrating and clearing out our vessel in pure love, have to be implemented. Challenges will continue to remain a thing of normality for us unless we do.

I can at this point begin to explain these changes more universally in terms of dimensions. These are often talked about in Science. Science is aware of portals in time and space. They often refer to them as "worm-holes". Science is also aware that other dimensions exist in it. Science is aware of and refers to there being 11 dimensions. There are in fact 167 dimensions. Being truly in spiritual awareness of all that is, and the fact that we are the Universe, stardust in form, has moved us along in its understanding much quicker than science. But what it shows is that Science and Spirituality are beginning to work hand in hand with each other, and talking about the same things existing, they are beginning to merge. Portals, vortexes and super nova's are things that exist and function in both spaces. Without the super nova, otherwise known as the death of a star, people could not exist. Scientists like Professor Brian Cox, openly say with gusto, that when a star implodes and dies, all the compounds, elements and minerals that create a human are put out into the atmosphere. What they haven't done, as yet, is state that it is the elements created from a dying star that actually makes up a human. This is an awareness that comes in, once you begin to function as the spiritual being that you are. Of course the same occurs in reverse when a human dies, the compounds that make a star are released and a new star begins to form. We are the Universe.

Now what fascinates me the most about this, is that the scientists are speaking with the enthusiasm of it being new information. The truth is it is rediscovered information. We are beginning to remember all that we are, that ancient civilisations simply knew as a matter of course. Ancient Egyptians created astrology, and finding one's direction based upon looking at the stars. Navigation methods so natural to ancient cultures are still used today when we are lost without a compass for a guide. Ancient civilisations did not have the later invented compass, and yet still never got lost. The stars spoke to them, and they listened. In the cities we have today, we are lucky if stars are even seen. This is how disconnected from our source we have at times become. In the same token, all ancient civilisations knew that we were interconnected and could heal using channelled energy or manipulating the energy through treatments like Reflexology. Today they are turned to as a last resort by many people. How lost we have become! When you look at the facts even the first known humans, Neanderthals, though they could not speak one word - just make noises- could be creative and do amazing cave art. They often drew scenes of hunting with the animal caught with stars above it and around the hunters. Even they knew the truth of their source, and drew art to give blessings and thanks for having caught a good meal, clothing and housing insulation. They knew they were the Universe in form quite naturally, and they never wanted for anything.

This does bring up another topic around animals and meat eating. Traditionally from the dawn of man, we are hunter gatherers. All ancient cultures were so connected to the truth, of us being the Universe in form, and using all natural remedies for healing. Yes they ate plants and herbs for general sustenance, but also for healing. They also without question ate meat. Every single person absolutely has free choice as to what they do with their diet, but there is nothing wrong whatsoever in eating meat. Animals are sacred, that is true, just as we are sacred. We can learn much from looking at human origins and ancient civilisations. They hunted animals for food, clothing and shelter. Therefore animals were held in great reverence, yet they still ate them. Every time they were successful hunters they gave thanks to God and they gave thanks to the animal for giving its life for theirs. As long as there is reverence for all living creatures and we give thanks to them, all is well. If I was on safari and a lion decided to hunt me and was successful, good for the lion, he needs to survive as much as I do. Hunting for survival has always existed. I admit due to how closed humanity has become some aspects of animal treatment is to say the least less than adequate. This is because some of us have lost our ability to go within for our answers, and have lost the connection to our truth, and therefore have lost respect and reverence for ourselves, let alone another species. Through reconnecting the reverence and what it is all about respect for all creatures and all circumstances will return. This begins by following the heartfelt communication from within, rather than the human mind. Where there is heart, there is nothing but respect and reverence for each other, and all living things. It all begins with ourselves. Each of us beginning to peel the layers of pain from ourselves to find the divine within. The only thing we really have any control over is our self, so using the techniques mentioned, and seeking help if required, we can truly get back to the wisdom and truth of who we are in a modern age, and move forward in love.

This brings me again to speak of dimensions. We are at this present time, in the process of moving quite naturally from the third to the fifth dimension. Science is, in the third dimension, by degrees learning all there is to offer, taking us to the fifth. The spiritual approach gives the realisation that we are already there, and can be there absolutely NOW, simply by choosing that space, and being in the moment of it. In truth there is never anything present but the moment, so simply by believing you are in the fifth dimension, you are by default naturally there.

The "appearance" of having so many "challenges" in recent years, is because we are in fact missing out the fourth dimension. The shift from the Third to the Fifth Dimension is happening swiftly, so the clearing of all that we no longer require to take us forward, is happening in quite quick and dramatic style. Know that all your challenges are for your highest good. We are moving into a very beautiful space because of them. The Fifth Dimension is a space of love and shining. Karma no longer exists, and there is no right or wrong, as everything is looked at through a loving heart and eye.

All the methods that I have mentioned previously, make the transition from one to the other much more simple and easy. We are in the Fifth Dimension NOW, if you simply change your focus to the eyes of love. As I have mentioned all that you dream of already exists elsewhere, you just need to believe and attract it into your existence NOW. When you have achieved your dreams, you are fully in the fifth dimension, and in a space of pure heart.

When you truly love and respect the self, and see your value and worth, how can you fail to see those things in another? It is simply part of natural flow. This is what we are bringing in for ourselves, pure divine love for all people and situations, no matter what they do or are, including the self. A space where there is no judgement, fear, anger or jealousy, only love and acceptance, in the wisdom that what we choose to focus on we bring to us in miraculous ways.

Chapter Eighteen

⌒〜

We are at the moment in the glorious space of the "in between". A space where we are clearing out all that we no longer need. We all harbour "unkind" thoughts. We all get into a space where we occasionally need to throw a tantrum. The truth is though, during these times, we are now clearing out all those old personality traits, and ways we have been taught, or have been dumped on us by others. Once the moment, or experience is over, it is gone for good, never to be repeated. We can take a deep breath and feel the joy in the freedom of that any time we choose.

This is why going within and following your intuition is so important. The new ways work under self-focus, and working together as a collective. We are all at different stages of growth, and this is what makes the current time so powerful. Bring your power forward, by focusing on what you want, rather than what you don't, and moving towards playing through life, by following your passions. This is what we are here for, and this is what we are required to do to find our true happiness and space in the new world that is coming to be.

Each one of us is a teacher of something that no one else can teach about. So look into your passions, and follow the one that makes you the most excited to create your "play for life" role. Each of us is magical and each of us is miraculous. No one is more "special" than another. In fact the reality is there is no such thing as special. We are all equal, and here to teach everyone else about our magical "passion for life". There is no "work" only "play" in the new space. Do what makes you happy, and believe in yourself. You can be and do anything that your heart desires. Take the steps required towards it, as they appear to you. Once you start on the first step, the rest of the steps will come thick and fast, as you move towards your dreams. You will be so happy and full of joy once you make the shift into this space of loving "beingness".

The beauty of it is, that it is there for ALL to experience. Every single person. You cannot possibly go wrong. That in itself is such a freeing thing to know. So look for your "passion for life", instead of "work", and take action towards making it your income base. You are here to shine your passions in whatever way that comes to you to do so. YOU CAN DO IT!

Everyone is equal and deserving of fulfilling their dreams. We each have our own space in the picture of society, and that needs to be respected, but there is no "specialness". So whatever your passion is, or your dream life is, have a go at creating it. Make a step towards it, knowing that God and the Universe are fully supporting you to do so, and will provide all the guidance you need to achieve the dream. It is far better to take a step, and see what route, or indeed routes, open up to you, than sit procrastinating, or in the space of "if only".

Procrastinating, has actually never served anyone for the greater good. The regret that it creates is a worthless emotion, and that realistically isn't you. You are so worthy and deserving of your dreams. Begin today to take the steps towards them. Do your research. If there is more that you need to know, before you feel you can step out in confidence, take the relevant course. As long as you are moving towards it, the end result will always be what you desire, and so much more. You only ever know at any given moment, what you require to take you forward. So what you are given to visualise and focus on to achieve the dream, is still only a small part of what your outcome will be. The dream in reality is always more magnificent than following the vision to achieve it. So what is stopping you from taking that first step today?

Push through any fears, or ego based emotions of hindrance. Push yourself out of your "comfort zone", and begin to shine your light. There isn't a single person in this world who doesn't have these emotions come up before any step forward. The difference between those that succeed in their dreams and those that don't, is simply, the ones that succeed push out of their "comfort zone", and do it regardless. JUST DO IT!

The "comfort zone", that we humans adore to be in, is simply a box that we create in the human mind. It is designed to keep us small, and therefore away from our dreams. This is why, when those fear based thoughts come into the equation, we need to have the wisdom to push through them, and do it anyway. It is through taking charge of yourself and your life, that you will gain the power to do this more and more, and attract your dreams to you much quicker.

"Power" is an interesting word. Those in a 3D physical human space, will see it as being in control, and in charge of other people, and quite often a space in which you can tell others what to do. I tell you now … no one has the right to tell another person what to do. You can provide leadership and guidance to others, but never control them.

This actually brings me to the true meaning of power. To be powerful is to be truly compassionate of heart, and indeed provide that compassionate leadership and guidance for others. It is absolutely up to them if they take notice of it or not, and this is where the compassionate forgiving lovingness, of true power comes in. To be powerful is to be a wise and compassionate loving leader. This is the space that we need to begin to acknowledge as truly powerful.

To simply flow with what is provided to you through life, is an immensely powerful thing. To flow with all aspects of change as they arrive without any form of restriction or stagnation from the old space, takes you in tremendous leaps and bounds forward to an AMAZING life. Your life is always a picture of your thought processes, and experiences of yourself mirrored back to you.

Say for example, you find it difficult to trust other people... You actually find it difficult to trust yourself, and are projecting that onto other people. Everything is actually upside down, from what you thought it was. Those who look to blame others for what is appearing to be going wrong with their life, are in fact blaming themselves. As I have already said, you are only 20% responsible, for anything that happens to you. It is an important thing to learn that there is no blame for anything at all. To learn this is to remove nearly all obstacles out of your life.

Chapter Nineteen

Remember always that change is always a positive thing, no matter what walk of life or circumstance it chooses to make its appearance. We as a collective people are always, whether we realise it or not, in a constant state of transformation. No matter how that transformation is taking place, it is always movement forward and is for the better. Whether the transformation comes with a positive air, or the illusion of being negative, it is teaching you more about yourself, and the rest of humanity, to take forward with you, to use in a form of repair for all.

Anyone "stuck" in the old ways, will find it difficult to accept any form of change. This is not their fault. It simply shows that they aren't fully accepting of themselves, or aspects of their life. It is up to them to grab the bull by the horns and make changes that suit their own energetic vibration. You are here to be happy, so where happiness appears to be evading you, be brave enough to push yourself beyond the comfort zone, and make the necessary changes. You know by your feelings already what needs to change, so take the steps to make it happen.

Here I must bring your awareness to another point. Please note that I have never said that following your heartfelt feelings will have the appearance of being easy. Following the heart is a brave thing to do, as it can give the appearance sometimes of upsetting others. I tell you now, if others throw tantrums because you are doing what is right for you, it is even more of a sign that the relevant changes need to be made. If others respond adversely to transformation that feels right to you in heart, then they have become too reliant upon you to create happiness for them. This is incorrect. Every single person is responsible for creating their own happiness. No one has the right to cling to anything, or anyone else to create happiness for them. Where there is unhappiness in your life, be brave enough to make the change. Ultimately in the end, even if initially it may appear to be a bad move, it is always positive for all. It is positive as it will teach all involved to look at themselves and grow in a way that will make them happy. Whilst you fail to see the good in change you will only attract more to be unhappy about. So be brave enough to evolve. Flow with the times, and changes that come in, there can only be positive results.

I am not saying however, that we must be the perfect beacons of love and light at all times. This is an impossible achievement whilst we are in the space of shifting from one dimension to another. The reason for this is because we are evolving at different rates, and we are energetically connected to all people all of the time. So no matter how evolved we are, we are going to pick something up to clear on a daily basis. Always take the time to check in with yourself daily. As I have said before, 90% of our thoughts actually do not belong to us personally. In the awareness of this, it does naturally give rise to daily check-ins with self. Sitting with hand on heart and asking "What do I need to clear?" "Does this thought actually belong to me?"

This is a process known as discernment. To be dedicated to the process of discerning every response and thought, is a sure way to getting you to the "pristine vessel" as quickly as possible. You may be surprised what comes up sometimes in the space of discernment. Write down what comes up. Always keep the positives and what belongs to you separate from the negatives and what doesn't belong to you, and isn't yours. This is so you can learn your direction in life from the positives, and remove all that isn't serving by destroying the negatives, and/or breathing them out.

During this process of discernment, an action may come to mind, which you know may have upset another, apologise for it. The power of an apology, near or far is immense. Allow all that isn't serving to leave you. This is so you can be purely in the moment, which is an immensely powerful and all-knowing space to be in.

Each moment is a point of power, the like of which will never be seen again. So be happy in each moment, and seek things to be happy and thankful for. Gratitude is a sure way to have a fulfilled and happy life as quickly as possible. Give thanks for everyday and the wonderful moments experienced throughout it. When you live purely in the moment, you can only see things to be thankful for. There is no dwelling on the past, or worrying about the future, there is only joyful presence. Who in this world doesn't want that?

Living purely in the moment, initially takes conscious effort to achieve. Like all things, the more you do it the more natural it becomes, so give it time. Never punish yourself for how long it takes. Always be easy, respectful and loving of you. Every time something comes up that takes you away from your "present moment" space, say thank you to it for showing you what you need to clear to find that Buddha like peaceful loving state of being, that is the true you. Remember, you are a soul having human experience, so in your truthful real state of being there is only peace and love for yourself and all living things.

When things come up for you that take you away from your present moment, let go of them in whatever way works for you. Writing it down, and destroy it, breathe it out, or affirm the joy in your life whilst looking in the mirror, or if you desire, take the time to do all the options. You can affirm things like "All is well in my world. I lovingly let go of all things that take me from my loving peace of heart. I know I am always safe and lovingly being in the present moment".

Chapter Twenty

⟋⟍

I wish at this point, to bring your attention to children and animals. They are always in the moment, and never have any worries or concerns. Yes they make mistakes. Yes they get upset over things and can throw tantrums, but they are over with and forgotten as soon as they started. Animals are from the same source as people. There is no separation. We have created separation through a "superiority complex" that we have created. Every living creature is the same in its origin. We are all, including animals, the Universe in form. This may appear a strange concept for some of you to grasp, that we are all created in the same way. This imaginary separation between human and animal has become strongly engrained. We are though, human and beast, stardust experiencing restriction on Earth. Animals and children embody how all humanity should be. Freedom and complete expression of who they are, in confidence, is the norm for them. They are also champions of the "less is more" philosophy. Both animals and children can sleep up to 16 hours a day. In this time they are growing, learning and expanding in their wisdom, as well as physically growing, and playing amidst the Universe that they are. Animals and children therefore, are as much teachers, as any adult human. Through observing them, we can learn so much about being in the moment, and going with the flow of everything that comes to us in our life. They have no other way of being. They simply naturally are in this joyous space, so through observing them, we learn so much. Yes, sometimes they are unruly. This is where they naturally teach us the need to create boundaries and protection for ourselves. Whatever we are observing from them, they are teaching us what we need to move forward in a respectful and unconditionally loving way. This is the state that we need to get back to. It is our true state, the state where dreams happen, if we give them joyful positive focus at all times.

Have you ever noticed that those adults, who are at the top of their field and extremely successful in all areas of life, have dreamed of doing their chosen occupation from the age of around five to seven, and have never seen themselves doing anything else? Hmmm… doesn't this confirm everything that I have written thus far?

Some of these "young at heart" successful people, have even faced strong adversity from their parents and peers, but they have remained powerful. That dream of being an actress, singer, physicist, entrepreneur, or whatever occupation it is for them, has never been wavered. They have stuck to their guns, stood in their power, and seen no other result. The outcome being, they become one of the top of their chosen field, highly respected and loved for all that they do.

If you feel you have lost this level of connection to yourself, you can always regain it, simply by being powerful enough in yourself to listen to your feelings and gut instincts, and push for what you want for yourself. No matter what blocks other people may try to put in the way to stop you, or indeed how your human "mind talk" may try to stop you, you can always push through them and achieve your desired outcome for you.

It is that self-love, self-trust, self-belief, and self-worth that takes us to our dreams. Giving the dream more focus than the negativity of others, is what achieves them for us. You pushing on regardless, and remaining in your own personal space, will move mountains and make it all happen for you. Always believe in you.

I would like to take the time to give animals a little more focus. We can learn a great deal about how to be from them. No species is more superior to another, just as no person is more "special" than another. This viewpoint of superiority, has come in through our "mistake" in looking outwards for our experience. When we actually take the time to look at the facts, we can see that we are actually striving to be like animals. Many of us love them dearly, and love having them around us in our daily lives. They teach us to be unconditionally loving, as no matter what we do, say, or complain about to them, they will only ever respond with a listening ear and adoring eyes. The beauty of them is that they never take anything on board. They listen and give an incredible level of love to us, unconditional love, and yet remain completely detached from what we are expressing. In the new space that we are moving into, we will actually become more and more like them, as actually it is completely serving to us to do so. It is a way of being that allows us to remain in our own power, and yet immensely loving to all around us. Animals are teachers to us, in this regard. They remind us, of where we truly come from, and show that we are the same, and from the same source, just materialised in a completely different form. We can learn much from being in their presence.

I have always found it most odd when people say they don't like animals. To me they are simply saying that they do not like themselves, and are projecting it onto that animal, or group of animals they don't like. For example, dogs are incredibly loyal, so a person saying they don't like them, tells me they have loyalty issues. A horse is incredibly powerful, so a person who fears them, fears the strength and magnitude of being connected to their true power. A creature that many fear is the spider. It is associated with magic and inspiration. The many legs they have scare people. Many see success as being a straight decisive line. It is not, many routes are taken before success is reached, like the eight legs of a spider, there can be many ways to receive the desired outcome. Unless though you take the steps, whether there be one, or eight, or more, you will not achieve the goal. Many who fear the spider, fear pushing out of their "comfort zone" and experiencing the magic it can bring them. I used to be terrified of them. Now I say hello to them, and happily share my space with them. Animals teach us so much about ourselves, and where we are at, by how we respond to them.

The truth is though we are from the same source, and contain within the wisdom of the Universe as we are all stardust. How at peace animals are with themselves. How they just instinctively know that they deserve the love they give us back multiplied. They know that certain responses from them will get certain responses from us, and all from a loving heartfelt space. Did you know that animals have the ability to live as long as humans?

Many people do not realise this. The reason they do not live as long as humans, is because they are always absorbing and taking away our pain, so we can get closer to our happy heart centres. They are natural healers and selfless loving beings. This is why they are even willing to stay in abusive situations, and never attack the person that hurts them. They only ever show compassionate love. This is because they see the loving soul within everyone, even their abuser, and will still be that little healer and absorb as much pain as they can, until they are spotted and rescued from the situation. No matter what adversity is thrown at them, they are only ever beacons of love, and divine protectors. We can learn much from observing them. They are, no way, in any shape or form less than us. They are also our teachers. This is why so many of us have such respect and love for them. We see their loving souls as much as they see ours.

Yes, animals do have a soul. They too are souls experiencing existence on Earth. It is an illusion created by religion that says they are soulless. Religion is in fact manipulated truth shaped to control humanity. There is nothing real about it. This is why certain elements of it are beginning to struggle and slowly die out. As people look to create their own happiness and dream life for them, the need for outside controlling influences, are becoming less and less, as we are taking charge of our own reality and truth.

Chapter Twenty-One

〰

I have referred to God many times in this book. Some may have felt uncomfortable with this, simply as they have been made to see God from a religious perspective. Indeed in my youth, I was raised a Catholic, so I know all too well how people can be led to see him. The truth of the matter is, God is the Universe. There is no box that you can put God into. God is everywhere. We are made in the likeness of God. This is why I say that we are the Universe in form. In the heartfelt wisdom that this provides, know that you also can never be put in any form of box. You are a free spirit. We are stardust, the Universe and God in form, souls having human experience, and therefore have no form of restriction. We are as a collective truly limitless. We are creative multidimensional beings. Any problem that you experience, can be solved by being creative in any way that flows to you from the heart core centre of your being. Even if what comes to you appears to be completely mundane, or the smallest of things, follow it and take that action. God cannot fill in the "how's" for you if you do not act on your creative impulses. The smallest action can have the most magical results. Never miss an opportunity to shine out who you are. Be the "yes person" that your soul's impulses invites you to be. It is a sure way to achieve your dreams.

The only restriction that we actually have to our progress, is the wonderful human we have created to house us. Therefore, if we truly accept and realise that we are souls having human experience, we can push through any human barrier that is provided to achieve our goals. God and the Universe want you to succeed, in everything that you wish to achieve. So as long as you are taking the steps towards that dream, God will always fill in the magic that creates the miracles to make it happen. Any fears and doubts around your magic that appear, push through them, knowing that you are good enough and worthy of the results that you envision. Also, let go of any thoughts of jealousy towards another. There may be a number of us on very similar journeys. This is a good thing. We are all here at the same time, as we are required at the same time. Know that there is always enough for everyone, and that you are completely safe. You can even take the time to breathe in that safety every day, and breathe out all that doesn't serve you. You can consciously breathe in, actually thinking "I breathe in love and safety of self", and as you breathe out you can think "I breathe out all that doesn't serve me". It may appear a small thing to do, but it can have very positive effects on you, and how you take action and move forward in life. Make the time to do it each day with your visualisation and meditation work, which I have mentioned previously. You are worthy of this healing time for you, so make it.

There may be people around you on very similar journeys, know with confidence that no one is on the same journey. Yes, we are all part of a collective, but also in our own spaces, with our own unique gifts to pass on to others. What is unique to you, will always be unique to you, and no one can ever take what you specifically can offer from you. This is why jealousy is an emotion, which tells you more about you, than it does about others. If you do feel jealousy pangs ever, write them down. What are the jealousy pangs around, and how do you respond to them when they arise. Look the writings over, and see what they actually tell you about you and where you are at in the current moment. In the knowledge of what it has taught you, you can destroy the writings, believing that you are removing that issue from you forever as you do. You can actually perform this exercise with any negative emotion that comes up for you. It will allow your soul to truly come forward and allow your creativity to express itself, and your life purpose to shine out of you, if you do. There will always be the appearance of people knowing more than you, or less than you, in whatever field you choose to practice in. That is just the way it is. Others, however, are none of your business, and in giving them focus you are only hindering your own progress and play for life. You have a uniqueness about you that no one else possesses, and shining that unique you out to the best of your ability, is the best and sure way to achieve your dreams and more. Just keep your eye on your journey, and allow your creativity to flow, as and how it comes to you. Even if it may seem utterly bizarre at the time, take the action, it has come to you for a reason. Whatever happens, as a consequence of the action, you will be full of gratitude for, as it has been part of what has taken you to your dreams.

If you ever do take the time to look back and gaze briefly at what you have learned from your experiences, you will see that actually all that you have required at any given moment, has always been there, whether you realised it at the time or not. This is pure truth. You always, without a doubt, always have what you need, just when you need it.

As humans we may worry that we are lacking what we require, and stress and worry about things. But in this brief space when we look back, we can see in the wisdom we now have that we have actually passed through any issue that has arisen, unscathed, and the outcome has been totally correct for your journey.

We can see when we take the time to briefly acknowledge the past, that whenever we require something to take us forward, it is always provided just when we need it. This is why being in the moment, all the time, and powerfully making each moment precisely what we desire it to be is so important. The more flowing and in the moment we are, the sooner we attract what we want, and create our dreams in form. This is a truthful fact. It is important to note though, even if we allow restriction and stress to take a hold of us in human form, if the outcome desired is meant, a miracle will always happen just at the perfect moment. This is because, no matter which space we are in, loving flow of soul, or restriction of human, we will always get what we choose to focus on as a result. The restrictive way, though is always more nail biting and much slower than following the loving flow of soul.

Chapter Twenty-Two

Everything is always about going within, being in the moment, and following your feelings of heart, gut instincts. Your desires can come to you within a click of a finger in this space. It does, however, take practice, like everything, to get to that level. As long as you are taking action towards releasing all old patterns of restriction, you can always get to this level of speed in achieving your goals.

Always stay happy and follow your joy. Any other feeling that comes to you, say no and move to where you heart says yes.

The ability to say no is extremely powerful, and is essential to keeping you on your track and in your personal space. If done from an assertive space of heart, it is in no way offensive. If you are being made unhappy about something, you have every right to say so. As long as you are respectful of the person you are saying no too, there will always be a peaceful outcome for all involved. Always stand in your power. Be yourself, be respectful, be loving in all situations, and in all responses.

Take charge of your destiny. You know by your feelings what is right for you. Never be ashamed of who you are, or the fact you may wish to move in a different direction from those around you. They are having their own life, their own experiences, their own learning, and you are having yours. Where your journeys do not work together, simply move away from the person, and that part of the journey, and be content to find your own space in the journey of repair for humanity. You are only here to fulfil your own journey, no one else's, so follow you guidance, and your guidance alone.

Following your guidance, and having the courage to say no, when things aren't feeling right to you, can give you the illusion of being very alone at times. The truth is, we are never alone, as we are all connected to each other energetically. You can never actually be alone. We are omnipresent, and can be everywhere at the same time. We share challenges and experiences, even though they may appear to us physically in entirely different ways.

Experiences that appear "negative", in reality, actually show us that we are on the right track. They are there to teach us what we need to know, for the magic that is ahead. Even, if the outcome seen from following an initial provided route appears to be correct, if it is too soon for it to manifest for you, a challenge may be provided to give you essential lessons, before it is time for that dream to become reality. However a route provides, it is always the right one, and is always ok. Be brave enough though to follow your truth. Act on your no impulses as much as your yes. The better at this you are the faster your dreams come true.

We are always in constant flow, so whatever we have at any given moment, in regards to our dreams unfolding, depends on how evolved we are in the new ways of being. How much we look inside, instead of outside ourselves to achieve a dream, dictates how quickly they come to us, how many challenges we have on the way, and how quickly it manifests in our physically reality.

It is simply always a matter of remembering. In order to switch from the old ways of being to the new ways, we just simply need to remember we are already there, and it is just simply; looking at everything from a higher perspective. What do I mean by "Higher Perspective"?

To look at things from a "Higher Perspective" is to look at everything from a positive angle. More often than not it consists of turning everything you know in your human space completely on its head. This is where solutions to every problem that you will ever have, whether it be personal, or worldwide will be found.

This is why it is so important to be yourself, and in your personal space. If anything outside of you becomes a main focus, take the responsibility that you have made that choice. Everything is a choice. You are responsible for how your life and experiences appear to you. To create your perfect life, simply focus upon yourself, and what you require to achieve it. Always be in your heart space without any form of ego. "Higher Perspective" comes naturally, when you take charge of your own life and creating your dreams in form. Anything working against you, move away from it. Keep on your track, your own journey, and follow your intuitive guidance to creating your life. See the good in everything. You are not manipulated by outside circumstances, unless you give them focus, and choose to let them effect you. You are your own master, and in charge of your own ship. Take responsibility for your part, even though it is only 20%, in everything that happens to you.

In the "Higher Perspective", everything is good and positive. Even if it initially appears to be totally against the journey you are creating for yourself, it is positive. The outcome in the end will always be everything you desire and more. It is important though that you take responsibility for your part in all things, and forgive yourself for any "wrong" that may have appeared. Forgiveness comes, and the ability to move forward with ease and grace happens, when you take full responsibility for your part in everything that happens to you. As I have said, you are your own master, and when you realise that and take good care of yourself, you will know that you are always safe, and that the positive outcome you seek, will always be your outcome in this space of loving responsibility for you that you have created. Keep your loving focus until your dreams are achieved for you. It is all about realising that you are on an adventure. You are a soul, simply discovering what it is like to be restricted. We created the human body we house, to provide this restriction. The "Higher Perspective" is all about realising, that we are truly limitless, and here to push through our human barriers, to achieve our dreams in life. The adventure human life brings is provided through realising this. In this realisation, everything becomes play. Trying everyway that comes to us through listening to our body's messages, following the feelings of joy, until what we envision is achieved for us. It may take a number of stops and starts, but as long as we continue following the joy and are heart impulses, we will always achieve the outcome envisioned. We can never in any way fail, as long as we follow the flow to the desired outcome. We can be and do anything we choose. How awesome that is.

Chapter Twenty-Three

What can be done, if you are a person that has been influenced by outside situations and responses, and lost your way?

Well the first thing to do is begin to become detached. For those that have been totally absorbed in the stuff of others, this can appear to be difficult initially. It means that you need to step back and become an observer of the world around you. It also means becoming an observer of yourself. It is all about giving yourself focus, respect and love. When you can do this for yourself, it naturally filters out among everyone and everything around you. It naturally raises vibration, as it doesn't allow you to be dragged down, or into, anyone else's "stuff". It is all about protecting yourself. See yourself daily, protected by a divine white light, bring it around you from the moment that you wake up. If you are unsure how to do this for yourself, ask God to protect you throughout each day. When you and God work together as a team, magic and miracles can take place for you daily. Never be afraid to ask God, or indeed the angels, for protection. You can ask them as many times as you like. They are everywhere, omnipresent, so can never be overburdened. They can be with everyone at the same time, so never be afraid to ask them for help. They cannot give assistance to you, unless you ask for it, so make sure you do. In any situation that you feel unsure about ask God and the angels to show you how you can move forward. Also, be aware of signs. White feathers from out of nowhere, for example, can often be signs that you are protected. I have always found it interesting that white feathers were given to those considered cowards in the WWI. The cowardice view is the human view. The souls view is that it was a symbol of protection for the peace keepers. Their focus on peace, is indeed to be commended. It is the "higher perspective" of the situation. We as humans, in warfare situations, actually do things the wrong way round, and focus on the wrong things. We have anti-war protests, which actually gives focus to war, and actually attracts it. In our heartfelt soul space, in the "higher perspective" we have peace rallies, which attract peace and harmony into the world instead. So a form of protection therefore, is to always be mindful of where your focus is. Do not allow yourself to get involved in other people's viewpoints in any way. If people come to you talking about problems, simply give it back to them, "Well what do you want to do about that?" Never allow yourself to get dragged into a conversation on other people's stuff. Chances are it probably has nothing to do with you, and probably may not even be based on a viewpoint anywhere near yours. Stay detached from it, and give them their power by asking them to provide ways and actions to solve it themselves. Your detachment, and allowing them to act for themselves, without getting sucked in, is immensely powerful for all involved.

An excellent place to start in the art of detachment, is moving away from things like the news programmes and newspapers. It immediately allows you to focus on you, and the way you wish the world to be for you. If someone begins to talk to you about what is going on in the outside world, it is perfectly ok to let them know that the outside world is no longer a thing of influence over you. It is perfectly alright to be assertive, and tell them from a loving space of heart, that you do not wish to give the negativity in the world any power over your life. In doing this you are also giving the first step in awareness to others, the realisation that they are in charge of their own experiences, and do not need to be influenced by others in creating their outside view of the world.

Fear, anger, jealousy, and any other human emotion comes in when we are not caring enough for ourselves. What can be done to begin to remove these feelings from us?

Self-care and self-love are so crucial in this. Our human bodies are 70% water. Therefore, hydration is a key factor, in keeping us in our space, and not allowing the human emotions to take hold of us. Increase your water intake. Fear, anger, jealousy etc. come into our experience when we are dehydrated. One way to combat these emotions then, is to drink more water. We are meant to drink a minimum of 2 litres of water a day, which is 4 pints or 8 half-pint glasses. Coffee and tea are not included in this. They actually dehydrate you. Herbal tea and hot water are included as they are alkaline, and therefore hydrating. This simple increase in water intake does so much to take you to yourself, and seeing the positive view in every experience.

Some become teetotal, so they can have constant pure joyous fluidity as their experience. That is their choice. I am by no means saying that if you drink alcohol you should stop. Everything has a place, and if you enjoy a tipple you can indeed continue to do so. On one level it is a protector, as it keeps you grounded and keeps you in your own space. It does allow things to come up that require to be released from you. It also has the ability to stop the more aware amongst us from seeing you from a distance. Having said that, too much can be detrimental to your human's physical health, if you haven't yet mastered the art of self-healing. Further, too much alcohol can totally detach you from yourself, and create behaviour outside the norm. Having said that it is totally your choice as to what you do, and no one has the right to tell you what your response to alcohol should be. If I am honest I enjoy a drink with friends and with food. Whatever your choice is it is fine. After all even Jesus drank wine.

All I will reiterate is that if you dehydrate yourself and do not take the time to re-hydrate, you will experience more of those considered "negative" human emotions, rather than the joy and happiness of heart, which is your natural default position.

Take time daily for you. I am always hearing from people, "That is easy to say". Well yes it is, to deny that would be silly. I will reiterate something I have said earlier here though. How on Earth do you expect people around you to care for you, love you, and respect you, if you are not doing those things for yourself? In truth they simply cannot. Everything that goes on around you is a reflection of you and where you are at on your journey to self, and your focus on things. Through realising and accepting this, making time for yourself, should become second nature to you. Every moment is important so make it your own, and how you want it. It has tremendous positive effects on you and your life. Spend 30 minutes a day just giving yourself focus and loving space for you, visualising the life you envision, as though it already exists for you. Write down all that comes up in guidance, whether it be positive direction for your route forward, or things coming up, old patterns of being to be released from you. All things that come up to be released, breathe them out, so that they can never return to you. Take this time to empower you.

Before every meeting with a person and the start of every day take the time, to see the event and day precisely as you want it. See the reactions the positive vibes that you want, everything about it, before it happens, and believe the event has already occurred precisely as you have seen it. Take the time for this and see things unfold just as you want them. You manifest what you think about and focus on the most, so make it powerful and work in your favour.

You contain everything within you that you need to create your perfect life. In this wisdom make every moment work for you.

Chapter Twenty-Four

The art of becoming the detached observer all begins with the self. Everything does. It requires you to step back and truly see how you respond and react in different situations. The response that you have to anyone or anything, can tell you a lot about yourself, and where you are at and what requires healing in you. Have a pad with you at all times, and take the time to write down how you respond to situations that arise for you. What makes you angry? What makes you laugh? What makes you sad? What makes you jealous or frustrated? Also, take the time to observe what you actually do when you respond. Take the time to learn about you. Amongst the learning there will also be divine pearls of wisdom come through regarding your journey. Make a note of them also as they arrive. You provide the best solutions, and give the best advice when you approach a situation as an observer. This is an incredibly powerful way of being, as it is all seeing.

What some people do not realise, is that when you allow yourself to become involved in any situation, you are actually giving your energy and power away to another, and weakening yourself. In this realisation, it becomes imperative to take charge of yourself, and keep your energy and power for you. You are always responsible for 20% of what happens to you, so accept that responsibility, and take the steps to remain at your most powerful.

Once you have truly taken on board that you are a spiritual being, nothing can ever be taken from you that you cannot recreate for yourself in another way. As a spiritual being you are all powerful and loving. The detachment, that allowing yourself to become the loving observer creates, allows you to simply move forward with ease and grace, from any situation that can be created for you. If someone takes a step to "knock you flat" for example, so that they can shine from what they have taken from you, simply allow it, without giving any focus or care to it. You can create your dream another way, and the outcome of that change in ease and grace, will always be better than the initial path started upon. Changes happen to improve your experience, not take away from you. It is all about the "Higher Perspective" of looking at things.

When you look at the actual facts, every single human being is here for the service of all humanity. Every single occupation that exists is about serving another in some way. Whether you be a spiritual leader and mentor, nurse, lawyer, secretary, in the field of hospitality, cleaner, dustbin man, or any other occupation, including animal care, everything is about serving all other living creatures in some way. This is why there is absolutely no level of superiority. We are in fact all the same, individual yet connected, working to serve every other living creature. This is why ego can leave us and love can come in, and why detachment will take us forward so much quicker. In the realisation that actually we are all in a divine mission of service, no matter what we are doing in the world, the need to compete, be jealous or indeed show any form of fear or other emotion becomes obsolete. It also brings forward the awareness, that if indeed every single person is in service, there is enough for everyone and more. No one actually can lose. We are absolutely in a win-win situation.

This is the "Higher Perspective" of human life. If every single person is in service, what is the point in doing something that doesn't bring you joy. How does that serve you or anybody else? Truthful fact… it doesn't.

This "Higher Perspective" viewpoint, also makes us aware, that it is absolutely right to give time to the self. If indeed we are all the same, just filling in our own individual space in the mission of service to all, what is the point of doing anything else other than focusing of repairing the self-first? Even in repairing the self, you are raising the vibration of all humanity, as you are serving you, which without question puts you in a better position to serve everybody else. You cannot give people what they truly need from you, whilst you are unhappy in yourself. Fulfilling Dreams happens when you feel fulfilled and happy in all ways right to the very core of your heart. Whilst you have any form of "stuff" going on within you, how can you truly expect to serve another to the best of your ability? The truth is you can't.

This is how we have become lost in our direction. We began to collect "stuff" within ourselves. Because we forgot to take care of ourselves, we began to pass it on to others. As the wonderful world we live on is becoming smaller, and all people are able to move about so freely, everything has been spread around, and we have become shadows of who we were.

It is wonderful to think that we can achieve the same with world repair. As we take the time to repair ourselves a bit at a time, we are also taking that around the globe with us, raising vibration, bringing repair and happiness as we go. What a magnificent thought.

Take the time to really look at yourself at this time. Are you happy? Which areas of your life aren't you happy about? What will fulfil you and bring you happiness in your mission of service? What do you really want to do to assist yourself, and every living thing around you?

If you currently are not happy in what you do for a living, begin to see it as a means to achieve a dream. Begin to take the steps no matter how small to make that dream happen for you. If you are wishing to bring about change, take the focus away from what no longer serves you, or brings you happiness, and begin to move away from it. You can make any change that you wish to make, as you can see there is absolutely nothing to fear. There are people waiting to serve you, to take you to a space of fulfilling your dreams. Simply just believe and know that you can make any required changes with ease and grace.

I am always fascinated to note that many people contact me for appointments, in the midst of their "Sunday Sorrows". So many people, dislike the prospect of getting up for "work" on a Monday. My brother even has a Garfield toy wearing a t-shirt that states "I hate Monday's". Oh dear…This is a space that no longer needs to exist. If you are in anyway unhappy with what you do, begin today to take the steps towards your happiness and fulfilled life. You are worthy and deserving of it. There is absolutely no point whatsoever staying in a space that isn't serving you. You will not be serving the rest of humanity in a way that is fulfilling to either of you. Love yourself enough to make any changes to bring about your perfect life for you. We are all the same after all, we are all here to give service in the way that makes us happy. So if you are not happy, take the steps towards that happy life you have always envisioned for yourself, and do it NOW. You are good enough, and you are deserving of it.

Remember, if it has ever appeared in your mind, it already exists for you, and you just need to bring it into your life, by focusing on the self, and what you see you need to do to bring it in. If you have seen it in your mind, you cannot possibly fail to bring it into your reality. You are, and have, what you decide to give the most focus too in your life. So give your perfect version of you, and your perfect life the most focus. Love and give thanks for everything around it, and as you take the steps of self-repair to bring it in for you. Say thank you thank you thank you, as at first the small, then the large, then the huge dreams begin to come in to your life. Give focus to the best of the best for you that you have ever seen. You just simply can't fail to bring it into your life.

Chapter Twenty-Five

I am now drawn to discuss the subject of boundaries. These are crucial elements to the spiritual being. Boundaries are a powerful thing. They allow you to stand in your power, and never let any part of who you are be taken from you. They give you the wonderfully powerful ability to say no, in any situation that doesn't agree with you. They give you the power to be assertive from the heart.

It is an all too common occurrence amongst humanity to go along with the majority vote, whether it agrees with you or not. This immediately puts you in the situation of giving your power and energy to another, as you have not taken charge of the situation and spoken your truth. Say for example, a group of friends wish to go to a restaurant, but it isn't actually a favourite of yours. It is perfectly ok to stand in your power in this situation and be assertive. You can simply do this by saying "As much as I like the restaurant that you wish to go to, I would prefer to go to… if it is open for discussion" You may get the majority vote in the end, but you will never know that unless you say. If you do not get the majority vote, then you have the choice to go or not. In this situation, do not go with what may please others, go with what feels right to you. Believe it or not you will gain the respect of the group for standing in your power, even if it may not initially appear that way. You will have taken the steps to be assertive, and therefore shown the rest it is possible, and they will at some point, even if not straight away, step up into the space you have made for them to do so. You have created a powerful boundary for yourself. You have shown you will not be walked on. This is a boundary that needs to be brought into every area of your life. For example, if you are at work, and you are asked to create a programme, take on the task, if it feels right to you, as it will only boost your position and morale. However, take notice of the wording. If they say "You can write a programme now, so that I can use it", this is an entirely different situation, as they are actually taking your power away from you in this instance, by "using" you. Here you have absolutely every right to stand in your power and be assertive. "Yes I will write a programme, but only if it is for me, and for me to deliver." This is self-respecting and therefore, should be taken notice of. Take good notice of the response from the other here. If they throw a tantrum, and try to make you out a demon, as you won't play their ball game that is their problem. It is nothing whatsoever to do with you. It never has been, and it never will be.

In this kind of situation, if someone throws a teddy into the corner, then it is all about them and where they are at. It never has been and never will be anything to do with you. This again is where detachment comes in. You can always say "I have been asked by someone to do a programme for them", you may find if you remain powerful and do this, that the other party was asked to produce something out of their depth, and they were looking to cover it up. Whatever the outcome of being assertive is, you can rest assured it will be the absolutely right outcome for you. In that knowledge, you can realise, that there is never any need to be afraid to follow your intuitive instincts. Whatever they are follow them. They are the true guide to your happiness and dreams. Boundaries and assertiveness are essential elements to creating true happiness and respect in all areas of your life.

I will bring in another important thing here, that works hand in hand with boundaries, and that is protection. In saying this, I do not mean you are required to walk around permanently with a body guard. I am referring to another way to hold onto your power. I have referred to it before, and there is no harm in reiterating it. There are a number of ways to protect yourself. As I have said before if God is in your life you can only ever be safe. You can ask him each day and night to protect you, guard you energy and power from others, so that you can move forward in ease and grace with more fluidity throughout your life.

Whenever you are feeling weak or in a space that isn't serving, ask God for protection. Really ask him for it, command it. He is omnipresent, and with all people, in all situations, all of the time. Ask him to protect you, so your path cannot be manipulated by another. Remember you are sailing your own ship, and in charge of your destiny. You have absolutely every right to ask for protection as you do it. God and the angels are there and with everyone every day and night. They are happy and never overburdened by anything that you ask of them. However, it is important to note, they cannot help you unless you ask them, so make sure that you do this. Every time you are feeling weaker than you feel you should, ask for them to help you. You will notice the difference instantly. Make it a part of your daily routine to ask for protection, and guidance throughout the day, in the direction of your dreams. Listen and trust your intuitive gut instincts. Know that your first thought is the right thought always. Listen and act upon your intuitive guidance as soon as it is received, don't wait, it has come for a reason, so trust it and act upon it. The more you listen and clear out what is no longer serving you, you will become more and more sensitive to situations and the people around you. You will become unmanipulable as you begin to completely trust the "first thought right thought" philosophy. It is extremely important to have powerful assertive boundaries, and protection around you at all times. They will keep you pure and in a loving space, the space that is required for the service and repair of yourself and all of humanity.

Both Boundaries and Protection are crucial for you keeping in your own space. I for example, have made the mistake in the past of having neither. I was so open and just attracted everyone's thoughts and patterns of being that were around me. The reason I let go of boundaries and protection is because I was abused in a number of different ways. Both were completely ignored, so I simply stopped caring about having them, as they had been ignored anyway. This in a way was a wrong reaction. But in another way it can be seen as a right reaction, because it has given me the wisdom to tell you that they are crucial and must be implemented to keep you in your own space, and on your own journey without being influenced by other's energy fields. Seeing it as a right reaction, and a thing of learning to pass on to you, is the "Higher Perception" of the situation, which my heart is so glad of, as it has given me the ability to write this, to assist you on your journey, and explain the importance of boundaries and protection. You are precious and deserve to be you, and shine who you truly are without interference from others affecting your beauty.

Chapter Twenty-Six

⌒

Everyone without exception is a result of their upbringing. As a consequence, unless you come from a spiritual background, you are initially going to have to put conscious effort into creating boundaries, and/or being assertive, and protecting yourself. This is all ok.

Remember, all experiences that we have, even if they initially appear negative, are positive and can be life changing for the better, if the lessons are used effectively.

These things can of course be difficult to grasp, if one has experienced trauma. For example, they could have been adopted or fostered out or have experienced some form of abuse, or the loss of a parent in their childhood life. If anyone has experienced a traumatic event in their life, it goes without saying that they are going to find it difficult to create boundaries for themselves. This is because, they have been taught at an early age there is no point in having them. Any boundaries that they will have had in place for themselves, will have been completely ignored, and their trust in themselves and others completely violated. In these instances, they may require assistance to find their boundaries. This is absolutely ok. It is a powerful thing to seek help, as it shows you wish to move forward out of that space. I am here to help you. I have experienced abuse myself, so know exactly what it is to be without boundaries or protection, and how incredibly powerful it is to take that power, once given to another, back for you.

We are all here to learn and grow from what we experience, and help others from what we learn. All people are equal, all are powerful, and all have unique gifts to pass on to help others to grow. Each and every one of us is powerful and divinely beautiful. You have every right to claim the power back, that you were once forced to give to another, no matter what the trauma was for you. Never be afraid to seek and ask for help to overcome the effects of this, and claim your power back. Boundaries are essential in all walks of life. To have your own, and see them in another is a crucial element of self-growth, to being the best that you can be.

To have the ability to detach and observe the patterns and behaviours of others, is a sure way to create boundaries and protection for the self. People are always trying to take from one another, thinking it is a means to empower the self. I tell you now, it is not. In the new ways I have mentioned, that we are moving into, there is absolutely no value or worth in even attempting to take from another. You are here to walk your own path and journey, and yours alone. So empower yourself, create your own boundaries, and leave everyone else to do the same themselves, knowing that as you grow and serve yourself, you are raising the vibration of the world, and repairing those around you also.

If you have been hurt or traumatized deeply by another, know that it absolutely, on any level whatsoever, had nothing to do with you. You were in no way responsible for the actions of the other person. It was all about them and where they were at in their life. If they hurt you deeply, they were hurting themselves deeply, and projecting that out onto you in whatever form it took. It never ever on any level had anything to do with you. Doesn't this knowledge bring a wonderful shift within, a wonderful awareness that you can now let go of it, and truly move forward. Most importantly it brings in the possibility and the space to forgive yourself.

If you have been in any circumstance, where you have been deeply hurt, I am sure you will initially be looking at what you did, and what it was about you that made them hurt you like that. Now you know, without a shadow of a doubt, that it was nothing you said or did that caused it. It was all about them, and where they were at, and absolutely nothing to do with you.

Please let go of any self-blame that you have ever experienced around another's actions. If you did not know what abuse, manipulation, bullying or any other traumatic event looked like on the way to you, how could you have ever noticed that it was going to happen? In all honesty you just wouldn't have. How could you have noticed something and put a stop to it, if you never knew how it would appear or what it would look like in the first place? You couldn't. Stop punishing yourself for these events that happened to you. You had no control over them, they just simply happened. They were all about the other person.

In the wisdom of this space, you can finally allow yourself to let go and move forward from it. Take a deep breath bringing in love and forgiveness of yourself as you do, and breathe out all you have held onto regarding the event. Know as you do, deep in your heart, that nothing around it was ever your fault, but you are so much wiser because of it. Give thanks for the wisdom the event has given you. Know deep within you, that nothing remotely like it, will ever happen to you again, as you have now learnt the signs of its approach. In that knowing you have created a wonderful protective boundary for yourself, that will never be breached again. You will receive those powerful signals before the event even occurs, and act upon them. More importantly, you now have a tool that many around you may not know. In this wise space you have found, you can pass the knowledge on to others, so that they will never experience what you have. In passing on the wisdom you have within, to give this knowledge to another, you are automatically raising awareness, and the vibration of the world, above and beyond the pain, abuse and trauma that it has once experienced. Always positively make use of what you know, and what you have learned. There are more people than you realise in the world that are requiring to know the unique gifts you possess for them to learn from. In passing on your unique gifts and wisdom, you are improving the world more than you will ever know.

Chapter Twenty-Seven

⮌

Your unique gifts, your natural abilities and insight, which lie within you are there for you to capitalise on whenever you choose. We are all teachers of something. The problem is that human nature comes equipped with a destructive button. The "mind talk" has the ability to tell us we are not good enough. It also contains a button that unfortunately tells others they aren't good enough too.

In ourselves we can make the choice to push through and carry on regardless. I can tell you, when you have achieved your goal, what you will look back on the most, without exception, is those times where you have taken charge of your journey. Those times when all you have heard, is that you won't achieve it, and you have got yourself together and done it anyway, regardless of others opinion and your "mind talk". These are the times that will stand out to you the most. The times you have pushed on through the storms and obstacles and still achieved the dream, will bring the moments of pride and accomplishment to you. It is far better to have tried and failed, than to have procrastinated and be full of "if only". "If only" isn't serving to anyone.

If you can see it in your mind, you can at any time bring it into your physical world. This is because it is real, it already exists for you. All you have to do is believe in it in your heart. This belief in the heart is what merges what you know and what you have imagined in the mind. All you need to do is take the steps to make it happen. Get busy taking any steps that come to you that will take you closer to that imagined dream. Circumstances, chance encounters and coincidences cannot happen, without you getting busy. You need to get out into the world, doing things associated with your dream, in order to bring the reality of it into your life. It simply cannot happen without action and input from you. The steps maybe small and humble, but nonetheless they are steps that will bring magic and miracles into your life. Never waiver from the dream or taking the steps towards it. If you are a cleaner and see yourself as a rich lady sailing upon yachts and having cocktails every day, know that you can achieve it.

The trick is to act as though it already exists for you, even if it currently is far from the truth. See it in the mind and celebrate it every day with gratitude. Say thank you for it already being part of your life, and totally believe in it. Take every step no matter how humble and small it may appear. The smallest step can lead to the biggest magical leaps you have ever seen.

As you begin to see the smallest of dreams come true in your life, give thanks and celebration for them, as that will attract the bigger ones. Give thanks and celebration for those, and then you will attract the huge ones. Always see the outcome and give thanks before it is even there. It will make it real faster than you will ever know. It is all about believing in yourself, and knowing deep within you are worthy and deserving of it. Start today to visualise, even for just five minutes each day, what your dream is for you, and give thanks for its realness in your life. See only the joy of it being there, and allow your happy vibe, to allow God to fill in the miracles required to achieve it.

It is already real, already there, waiting for you to step up and attract it to you. You are a magical, infinite, multidimensional being that is truly unlimited. You can be and do anything you choose. You are a soul having human experience after all. You can have the humblest of starts, and end up with the richest life in every possible way. Just simply see it there for you, and believe you are deserving of it.

There is a certain element of pretence to creating it. It is like being the actor or actress of your life. Behave as though you are already living that life. Put out into the world your dream, and follow every step that comes to you to take you there without exception. It does need to be done with ease and grace however. Ego will not gain you many favours, so simply allow the ego to leave you. You are not better than anyone else because you attracted your dream. You possibly just gained the ability to attract the dream into reality sooner, but you are not better than anyone else. So let any emotions that say that evaporate, let them leave you. It is love that takes you forward now.

If you have achieved, or are achieving your dreams faster than another, then be in your heart space and teach others what you know, to help them step up to join you. Never rub anything in another's face, or take the 'look where I am' approach. Rudeness on any level is unacceptable, as it simply does not come from a loving heart space. Be willing to show people and share your secrets of success, whatever endeavour you have achieved. I tell you now, every single person on this beautiful earth, is so worthy and deserving of having everything they have ever dreamed of, in their life now. Purely and Simply BELIEVE IT.

Chapter Twenty-Eight

As a soul you are never ending, unceasing, immortal. The soul can never die. There are some incredibly wise souls here on earth sharing human experience with you. All exist to help each other to grow and achieve their dreams. What you do not know, or yet understand, take time to seek out the answer. There are mentors everywhere, which can take you forward. I can take you forward, just as in return you can take me forward. We all contain something unique to pass on to everyone else. In this space there is absolutely nothing whatsoever to fear. Humans currently are extremely fearful, and have attracted worldwide issues and events through giving their fear focus.

Many humans for example have issue with death. They fear it. In the wisdom, that you are a soul having human experience, and in that space are immortal, a whole new perspective comes into play. The restriction of the human body is something that you can come in and out of. You may have different human creations housing you each time, but you can come and go as you choose, to learn something yourself, to teach others something, or just share in the playful adventure that human life can bring.

It is true, that every night, in the deepest part of our sleep, our physical body actually dies, as the soul goes off to see what the completed dream you are making real for you looks like, or learn the next step to achieve it from God. Always give gratitude for every day that you experience. Your soul could have easily decided not to bother to return.

Many humans may have experienced trauma around death. They may have lost a baby, or a loved one in a terrible accident, or to terminal illness, and it appears to be all too soon. I do deeply understand these human perspectives, I have been through them. I have felt the pain and the loss on a human level. No one is immune to this. We love the human houses that we each make for ourselves so deeply, and love sharing our experiences with others around us. However, I have learnt in the experiencing of these kind of events, everything happens at the right time, and just as it should be. No one is ever given more than what they can handle or learn from. Each experience helps you to grow. As you overcome the trauma of the event, you begin to notice how you can help others to overcome similar circumstances. Some people may be stuck in the trauma, so if you have overcome and know some helpful tips that may help others to do the same, you can perhaps start a group to teach others what you know. Everything happens for a reason, even if that reason may be so difficult to see. Everything happens to help us to grow and help humanity as a whole to grow, by simply passing on what we have learned and the wisdom we have gained and know.

No matter what the situation is, whether it comes in a positive or negative guise, God is always present. This is where the "Higher Perception" comes in that I have touched on previously. Yes we need to grieve, and let all our feelings around a situation come up and release from the body, whether it be around warfare, death, loss of a job, or any other uncomfortable situation. In the wisdom that God is always present in everything that happens to us, we can be aware that there ultimately is always a positive result on the other side. The saying 'every cloud has a silver lining' is absolutely true. If you see something that you can do to help others from what you have experienced, be brave enough to step up and use it. It can only serve you and all those that experience what you can offer for the better. You contain a key through your experiences that can help all of humanity to grow, and ultimately raise the vibration of the world. In this wisdom, what use is there sitting and doing nothing about it... in truth absolutely nothing.

Know deep within the very core of you that you are magnificent. Know that you are capable of moving mountains for yourself and others by taking notice of everything that goes on around you and to you. By being the observer, even if initially you become completely engulfed and confused by a situation, you can on the other side, see what you have learned from it, by observing everything that you have been through in that time. You can transform your life and the lives of others if you can have the courage enough to follow through and teach what you have learned.

Never ever give up. Once you start something, follow it through to the end regardless of any obstacle. You deserve the best that is available to you, and you get it just by doing and pushing yourself all the time until you achieve.

You may have just retired and have realised that the breadth of your knowledge, is worthy of passing on to others. Whatever gift you possess within, pass it on, share it with the world. You are never too old to do anything. Remember you are infinite. Just simply act and do something with the magic you have contained within you.

You may be a young person, who has had a near death experience to share with the world, to prove that death as humanity knows it isn't the reality. Share it.

You may have been through trauma of some kind. Through becoming the observer you can see the strength that you have contained within you that others may need to learn from. Share it.

Whatever you have experienced in your life, somewhere in it lies the pearl, the uniqueness of you, your soul's pure innocent beauty that you can pass on to another to help them grow. Take the time to do it.

You can pass on what you know in any way you choose. Books, courses, music, there are so many ways open to you. Use the one that appeals to you the most and act upon it NOW. If the joy is there in your heart, act upon that joy, and what it is telling you to do NOW. You are here to express, share, teach and learn in whatever way appeals to you. Take the time to do it.

Know that if you are on the very start of realising your truth, it is a very powerful thing to seek help. Anything that helps you to grow in confidence to be yourself, is always a powerful thing for you to do. There are many out there, other than myself that can help you to grow, and gain your confidence in who you are. Do not be afraid to reach out. There are many mentors out there that can help you in many different ways. It is powerful to seek them out and learn, and then pass on your unique gift from what you have learned.

You as a soul are all powerful and infinite, and you have decided to experience being human to be of service to all humanity. Whatever, you can do to be of service to another, take the time to do it. Within you contain great wisdom, and something wonderfully unique, that you can take the time to teach another to be of service. You can simply see a man lost in the street, and help him find his home. Whatever action you take, big or small, to help your fellow human experiencers, know that it is taking you closer and closer to your ultimate destination, your vision that you see for your perfect life. Always therefore take the time to assist another, no matter how the way to assist may appear to you.

In your actions of service to humanity, do it in a loving and caring way, through love of heart and kindness. Never begrudge having to assist another. One day you may require the assistance for you that you have provided for another. Begrudge anything that you do for another, when you require assistance it may not be returned. Always serve another the best way you can, with a joyful happy heart. Do anything in gladness and love, God and the Universe will return it to you multiplied. When you assist another, God and the Universe assist you, and move you ever closer to your dreams.

You are so worthy and deserving of the life of your dreams. Take the time to make it happen for you, in whatever way feels right and appeals to you. Remember you cannot do anything wrong. Every direction that you take is the right one, and will ultimately take you to a positive result beyond your wildest dreams. Believe in yourself and act NOW. You are worthy and deserving of it, so DO IT.

Chapter Twenty-Nine

As I draw my first book to a close, I wish you to know deeply and completely the absolute reality and truth of who you are. I wish to leave you feeling inspired and empowered, and trusting of yourself and all that you are.

The most important point to take away with you is that you are a soul having human experience. You are the Universe, stardust in form. In the wisdom of this space you are deeply and completely an all knowing, infinite, multidimensional being. You are an 'Ascended Master'. What you are I am too, as we are all energetically connected. "I am that I am", is the truth of all that is.

We are always present and connected in a mission of service to all of humanity. You can be and do anything you choose. Nothing is right or wrong, as we are all connected and in service to repair ourselves and each other. Nothing can ever be taken from you. You may achieve the desired outcome in a completely different way to first envisioned, but the reality is, if you have seen it in your mind, it can be your reality. All it takes is for you to take steps towards it based on your intuitive gut instincts. Follow them to the letter, and have patience in there coming. Just simply know that all you envision and give the most focus too, will come to you, as that is what you are giving the most power too, and attracting through the law of attraction. Always give the most focus to positive steps and outcomes for you.

Be patient, and have belief and trust that absolutely everything is happening at the right time, and just as it should be. If you have impatience you are showing you are lacking in something. As a consequence impatience will actually push your dreams away from you rather than attract them closer. If you are putting out lack, you will attract more to feel lacking about.

Everything is energy. In this knowledge you know that what you have in your life, is always a reflection of how much you value yourself. So simply let go of all the egotistical and "negative" emotions, and trust yourself to always find your way back to you, and your journey to the perfect life.

All people are in service to all others, no matter what they do. Be brave enough to push through any barriers that arise to achieve a positive step forward for you.

Remember, simply having a dream, shows that you have courage. If you are seeing your dream as your reality in each moment, therefore bringing it to you, it shows you are persistent as well as courageous. If you are physically following your heartfelt feelings towards your dreams, you have tremendous bravery. If you are able to simply flow with your heartfelt feelings, and let go of any thought patterns of how to do it, this shows that you contain the infinite wisdom of the Universe. You were simply born to inspire, so get to it.

You are an 'Ascended Master'. You are truly limitless. There is absolutely nothing that you cannot achieve. So simply play the game of creating your dreams through restriction you have made by becoming human. Everything is an adventurous game, to achieve a dream whilst being in a human body. Believe, trust and love yourself enough to achieve everything you have ever seen in your mind. I tell you now you can and you will, the answer to any desire that you can ever wish to have or achieve is within you. Purely and simply follow your heart and gut instincts, and above all BELIEVE.

Printed in the United States
By Bookmasters